The Stanley Show

A review of the shows from

1878 to 1889

and the

1890 Show Review

(A reprint from the Irish Cyclist and Athlete, Thursday January 30th 1890)

The John Pinkerton Memorial Publishing Fund

Following the untimely death of John Pinkerton in 2002, a proposal was made to set up a fund in his memory.

The objective of the Fund is to continue the publishing activities initiated by John Pinkerton, that is to publish historical material on the development of the bicycle of all types and related activities. This will include reprints of significant cycling journal articles, manufacturers' technical information including catalogues, parts lists, drawings and other technical information.

Published by the John Pinkerton Memorial Publishing Fund, 2009
© John Pinkerton Memorial Publishing Fund 2009. All rights reserved.

ISBN 978-0-9560430-3-0

Scanning and layout, Brian Hayward, Printed by Quorum Print Services Ltd. Cheltenham.

INTRODUCTION

This monograph covers the very heart of cycle history. A review of the thirteenth annual Stanley Show, including a history of the previous twelve. A J Wilson (Faed) wrote it for the paper of his friend, the equally famous cyclist R J Mecredy. Wilson, not unkindly nicknamed Faed by his friends because of his deafness, funded the North Road Club and the Cycle and Motorcycle Trade Benevolent Fund as well as authoring several cycling books.

The dozen years spanning the 1880s are arguably the most exciting in the canon witnessing the swift rise and decline of the tricycle, the flowering and fading of the ordinary and the laboured birth and complex infancy of the safety bicycle.

It is revealing to have this period described by someone who famously rode most of the new machines of the period. Then, as now, the main trade exhibitions were where manufacturers showcased their ideas and this reprint will undoubtedly entice many readers into getting involved in the history of a fascinating era.

The development of the cycle industry during the period is indicated by this summary of the London venues and number of machines exhibited.

Date	Venue	No. Machines
1878	Camden Athenaeum	70
1879	Foresters' Hall	110
1880	Holborn Town Hall	150
1881	Holborn Town Hall	250
1882	Agricultural Hall	430
1883	Albert Hall	520
1884	Floral Hall	550
1885	Embankment	280
1886	Royal Aquarium	600
1887	Royal Aquarium	650
1888	Royal Aquarium	750
1889	Crystal Palace	1200
1890	Crystal Palace	1450

Nicholas Clayton
Honorary Member
Veteran-Cycle Club

Nicholas Clayton has kindly allowed JPMPF to completely reproduce his original edition of 'The Irish Cyclist and Athlete' of 30th January 1890. It gives an overall view of the cycle industry products of the 1880's. Also there is a host of fascinating advertisements to explore.

Cyril Hancock
Chairman John Pinkerton Memorial Publishing Fund

STANLEY SHOW NUMBER. SPECIAL EDITION OF

THE IRISH

Cyclist and Athlete:

The Official Organ of the Irish Champien Cycling Club, or the Dublin University Bicycle Club, of the Ohne Hast C.C., of the Newry C.C., of the Rovers' C.C., of the Fermoy B.C., of the Mossley B.C., of the Rugby B.C., of the Waterford B.C., of the Richmond B.C., of the Londonderry B.C., ot the Windsor B.C., of the Dungarvan Ramblers' B.C., ot the Co. Kerry Athletic and C.C., of the Sarsfield Gaelic C.C., of the Cookstown C.C., of the Limerick A.A. and B.C., of the Cruisers' C.C., of the Roscrea C.C. (the Ramblers), of the Cork C.C., of the Ulster T.C., of the Tullamore A.A.C., Gorey C.C., Pembroke C.C., Kincora C.C., High School B.C., Cork Gaelic C.C., Kerry B.C., Clonmel B.C., Zingari C.C., Ixion C.C., of the 4r C.C., Enniscorthy C.C., Ladies C.C., Round Tower B.C., Nenagh Cycling Club, Drogheda C.C., Y.M.B.C.A. Cycling Club, Coleraine Academical C.C., Killarney C.C., Carlow B.C., D Y.M.C.A.C.C., Dundalk Y.M.C.C., Tuam C.C., Munster Safety B C. Rathmines School C.C., Jurists C.C., Star C.C., Dublin Ramblers C.C., Belgrave C.C., and of the Irish Rifle Association.

N . 13 —VOL. VI.—Established May, 1855.]   THURSDAY, JANUARY 30th, 1890.   [One Penny

Notice.

" THE IRISH CYCLIST AND ATHLETE " is published every Wednesday morning at The Abbey Printing Works, 49, Middle Abbey Street, Dublin, and may be had of all Newsvendors, and Cycle Agents, Price One Penny ; or by Post—

Twelve Months, ... 6s. 6d. | Three Mon hs,   . 1s. 8d.
S x   ,, ... 3s. 3d. | Single Copy,   .. cs 1½d.

Payable in Advance.

Copies may be had in London from Iliffe & Son, 3, Bride Street, Ludgate Circus.

EDITORIAL.

Correspondents should address the Editor, 49, Middle Abbey Street, Dublin, and write on the envelope, Cycling, Football, Athletics, etc., as the case may be.

To secure insertion in next issue, letters should reach the Editor not later than Monday morning, and advertisements not later than Saturday.

Business Communications and Advertising Matter should be addressed to the Manager, " Irish Cyclist and Athlete at the Office, 49, Middle Abbey Street.

Cheques and P. O Orders to be made payable to the Proprietors, Messrs. R. J. Mecredy and S. Kyle, Dublin.

THE HISTORY OF THE STANLEY SHOW.

By A. J. Wilson. *

So thoroughly representative of the cycle trade in England is the annual exhibition promoted by the Stanley Bicycle Club, that a history of the Stanley Show is tantamount to a history of the development of cycle-building during the dozen years that have elapsed since the first of the series was held.

Few of the cyclists of to-day can realise the enormous strides that have been made during these twelve years in the manufacture of cycles ; and the contrast to the exhibitions of to-day, with their 200 separate exhibitors displaying two thousand machines, is typical of the advancement in the trade itself, when compared to the relatively microscopical nature of the first show, which was held in March, 1878, at the Camden Road Athenæum, some fifty bicycles being shown, mostly the property of the members of the club, and so little trade importance being attached to the affair that the report in *Bicycling News* occupied only a third of a narrow column. As an interesting comparison to the Stanley Show Number of The Irish Cyclist and Athlete, we subjoin an exact copy of this report :—

Stanley Bicycle Club.

The conversazione and exhibition of bicycles arranged by this energetic club was held last Tuesday and Wednesday at the Athenæum, Camden Road, and was a deserved success, upon which the executive may be fairly congratulated. At the commencement of the exhibition a beautiful "Timberlake" was presented to Mr. J. Robinson Airey, the popular captain of this well-known club. In addition to a safety belonging to the Right Hon. Robert Lowe, M.P., President of the West Kent Bicycle Club, there were many excellent specimens of workmanship in the room, including Mr. Blood's pony bicycle, exhibited by the Coventry Machinists Company, racer and roadster bicycles by Humber and Marriott, and machines from the works of Timberlake, Haynes and Jefferis, Grout, Carver, Hydes and Wigfull, the Surrey Machinists Company, and other eminent

* Copyright Reserved,

manufacturers. Several specimens of lamps, bells, and cther necessary appendages were on view ; and upon each evening well-executed music formed a pleasing part of the programme.

The safety bicycles referred to were the only safety machines in use at the time, the one being a lever-action rear-driver, the invention of Mr. Lawson, which was afterwards taken up by Singer and Company, and of which we append an illustration ; and the other, Mr. Blood's dwarf bicycle, with hanging cranks, a sort of unheared " Kangaroo " pattern.

THE FIRST SAFETY.

Even at this early date, anti-vibration contrivances were thought of, but the only one actually on the market was " Smith's Electric Vibrating Handle-bar,"

SMITH'S ELECTRIC VIBRATING HANDLEBAR.

which was made in halves, pivoted in the middle, and furnished with springs to allow vertical play of the

STAND 73.

Our leading patterns for the coming season are the following—

The Geared Facile.

Pronounced by many competent judges, including MR. GERALD STONEY ("Decimal Six"), the well-known authority on cycles, to be the best machine they have ever ridden.

THE FARRINGDON ORDINARY.

The leading "Rational" Bicycle. During the present year there will be a large return to the "good old ordinary," and riders will find it impossible to purchase a better machine than the "FARRINGDON."

The FARRINGDON SAFETY.

A high-class machine, at moderate price ; perfect ball-steering, improved and very rigid frame, patent detachable chain wheel.

Messrs. BOOTH BROTHERS, Ltd., Dublin,

ARE THE SOLE AGENTS FOR THE

"FACILE" AND "FARRINGDON" CYCLES,

And will be pleased to show them and give all information.

SOLE MANUFACTURERS—

Ellis & Co., Limited, 47, Farringdon Road, London, E.C.

ends. Structural defects interfered with its widespread adoption. The only tricycle shown was Starley's "Coventry."

STARLEY'S COVENTRY LEVER TRICYCLF.

The unexpected success of the first exhibition, and of an outside show at the Agricultural Hall in connection with a six days' race, led the club to promote one upon a more ambitious scale in the following year, the scene being the Foresters' Hall, Clerkenwell. Goy was the largest exhibitor, showing forty-four bicycles for which he held the agency ; and other prominent firms were Hydes and Wigfull— one of the chief makers of the time, who unaccountably dropped out of the trade without any indication of their intention—the Coventry Machinists Co., proud of their "all steel" club bicycle, and with a rear-wheel break which automatically applied itself if the cord broke. This firm also announced that they were putting down a plant to nickel-plate the bright parts of bicycles,—plating being then a recently-introduced luxury. Wicksteed's stand, Lamplugh and Brown's tool-bags, and the D. H. F. bicycle, were introduced, as was also the Facile bicycle. Carver's bicycle with hollow spokes created a great sensation, and Humber's front wheel spoon-break was greatly admired. Sparrow's invention of a strip of leather stuck upon the rubber tyre to prevent slipping aroused considerable interest, and Harrington showed a bicycle with balls all over. The appearance of the early ball pedals was very clumsy, the balls being carried in wide external boxes.

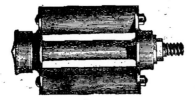

EARLY BALL PEDAL.

Gorton, of Wolverhampton, displayed a cyclometer which rang a bell at the completion of each mile, from which it would appear that Boys's "Signal" was not an original idea. The Salvoquadricycle was shown in all its original clumsiness,

STARLEY'S ORIGINAL SALVOQUADRICYCLF.

and several very imperfect tricycles and manumotives were exhibited. Aves's Pickwick bearing—a combination of coned rollers—was an ineffectual effort to stem the tide of the advancement of the ball-bearing. Most ingenious of all—although a commercial failure —was Grout's "portable" bicycle, constructed with joints enabling the large wheel to be divided into four parts, the backbone also being divsible, so that all would pack into a triangular "carpet-bag," enabling the bicyclist to travel by rail without paying for his machine.

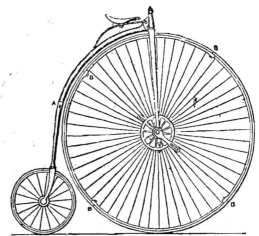

THE "PORTABLE" BICYCLE READY FOR USE.

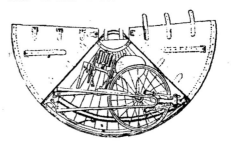

THE "PORTABLE" BICYCLE PACKED IN THE "WONDERFUL BAG."

A move to the Holborn Town Hall was made in 1880, but notwithstanding the increased accommodation considerable crowding resulted. A great advance

LINLEY & BIGGS
"WHIPPET."
Stand 41, STANLEY SHOW.

LADIES' TRICYCLE.

Write for Lists and "Practical Hints on Cycling."

LINLEY AND BIGGS,

Makers of the "Whippet" Cycles,

29, CLERKENWELL ROAD,

LONDON, E.C.

was shown all round in the finish of machines, and among peculiar features in bicycles must not be forgotten the " ratchet," or more properly rack-and-pinion, break, applied by twisting the handles round, on Timberlake's bicycles. Another peculiar break was the strap or band break on the hubs of the front wheel of the Arab bicycle, with which exception, and a solitary example of the old back-wheel break, the front tyre break was by this time universal, although a few makers fitted a roller to it instead of a spoon. The Arab bicycle already mentioned had its tyres fixed by a peculiar method, small hooks holding it to the rim between every spoke. All-bright bicycles were still the prevailing style, the firm of Humber and Marriott showing some very beautifully polished racers. Invincible racers were also popular. The Defiance bicycle, with an exceptionally strong but heavy arrangement to secure rigidity at the steering head, was much admired; and in the Desideratum bicycle the head nuts were altogether dispensed with, the coned top-centre of the steering automatically adjusting itself by means of a spring imposed between the centre-top and the closed head-top. Plowright's " Lynn Express " was enjoying fame by virtue of its exceptionally dust-proof roller bearings ; and the Centaur Co. introduced the double-fluted hollow fork. The Coventry Machinists Co. exhibited a 60-inch racer, built for Cortis, with a wonderful arrangement of eccentric sliding cranks which were to accomplish marvels in the way of speed ; but this, like every other eccentric motion, never came to anything in practice. A " Club " roadster with adjustable rake appealed to lovers of safety, a jointed arrangement of the head enabling its rider to increase the rake of his front fork by six inches, without checking his speed, thus reducing the probability of a cropper. Another contrivance to effect this result was the Centaur sliding saddle, having a frame jointed like a parallel ruler, so that it could be shifted back and forward at pleasure. Safety bicycles were represented by a crude specimen of the Bicyclette, and the Xtra, a

THE XTRA BICYCLE.

60-inch, built for P. G. Hebblethwaite, being shown, upon which that rider afterwards raced successfully at Stamford Bridge and elsewhere. Tricycles were fast gaining ground, and among those exhibited this year were the Devon tricycle, with its clever swing frame, which only went out of fashion two or three years ago ; the Coventry, with both lever action and its new rotary form ; Timberlake's telescopic tricycle ; the improved Salvo tricycles (including one for a lady, with 40 inch wheels, which were considered phenomenally small !); the cog-driving Excelsior and the chain-driving Flying Dutchman, rear steerers ; Starley's " Sociable " (trade mark) ; a lever action sociable, and the Centaur convertible sociable, convertible into a front-steering two-

THE FLYING DUTCHMAN TRICYCLE.

track single tricycle. Lamplugh and Brown showed a roller saddle, canting on each side alternately, and introduced tricycle saddles with back rests ; Dearlove electrified the wheel world with the first King of the Road lamps ; Newton, Wilson and Co. showed combination pedals, rubber one side and rat-trap the other ; a photo camera, on a Club tricycle, was a great novelty ; Hancock's tyres, and Harrington's Cradle-springs, were brought out ; a back wheel mudguard excited great surprise ; and one firm showed spokes " blued " to prevent rust. The hall and two side rooms contained the whole exhibits, accessories being accommodated upon the window ledges ; and a musical programme was again considered necessary to attract visitors.

The year 1881 found the Show again located at the Holborn Town Hall, additional space being utilized by covering-in the back-yard with tarpaulins, and the exhibits increased to 250 machines, of which no less than 67 were tricycles, the triple-wheel interest being now fairly booming, thanks to the good shows made in the fifty-miles road championship races, won first upon the Flying Dutchman and next (virtually) upon the Humber. Harrington's enamel was now all the rage, its effect being something far in advance of the inferior painting which had been customary previously ; and the great novelty of this Show was the " Baronet " steam-tricycle, exhibited by its inventor, Sir Thomas Parkyn ; its price was fixed at £45, but the law against using steam locomotives on the highway at a faster pace than three miles an hour prevented its being used. Curiosities in the shape of Gompertz's Hobby-horse, and

GOMPERTZ'S HOBBY-HORSE.

LAMPLUGH & BROWN.
STAND 220
For High-class Cycle Saddlery.

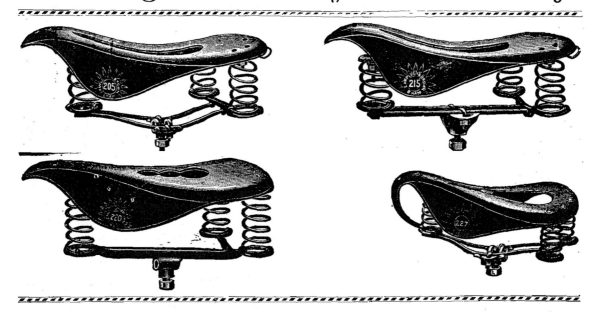

"PNEUMATIC"

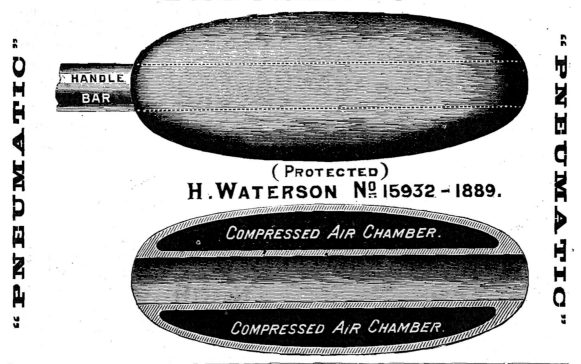

(PROTECTED)
H. WATERSON Nº 15932 - 1889.

COMPRESSED AIR CHAMBER.

COMPRESSED AIR CHAMBER.

135, Gt. Colmore-st., Birmingham.

Mr. J. H. Blackwell's collection of old hobby-horse caricatures, added their attractions to the show, but the musical programme was confined to a brass band. The ordinary bicycle was by this time settling down into a settled groove, ball-bearings being nearly universal, and Bown's ball-pedals being very much neater affairs than those previously made. M. D. Rucker made his first appearance as a cycle-builder, and the Swindley's patent steering-head fitted to his bicycles became popular. The Matchless rubber-cushioned bicycle was brought forward, and attracted considerable notice, being the most effective anti-vibration contrivance up to date, although Palmer's spring bicycle was a promising claimant for patronage; it had its back-fork hinged to the tail of the backbone, a flat steel spring controlling the jerks; a double-bow steel spring supported the saddle, and the handle-bar had forward play controlled by another spring. Another anti-vibration appliance was Wood's back-fork, the tail of which consisted of coil springs; and Woolley's Duplex saddle had a flat steel spring under its iron plate. A foreign maker—Truffault, of Tours—showed an ordinary bicycle with a pair of rocking levers in front of the handle-bar, designed to enable the rider to work with his hands as well as his feet in hill-climbing. Another hill-climbing idea was Garrood's Secondary Handles, which were made so as to be attached each to one leg of the front fork of a tall bicycle, a foot

BICYCLIST USING GARROOD'S SECONDARY HANDLES UP-HILL.

below the handle-bar, so that the rider was to lean over his handle-bar and, with a straight arm, pull at these low-down secondary handles. Gimlet, or T, handles were first shown; and the Pilot bicycle was the only one to have dropped ends to its handle-bar, although the Invincibles had cowhorned handle-bars. A small horn handle to the break lever was considered a great improvement, on the ground that the horn would not be so cold as steel, in winter. Weights were coming down, a semi-racing bicycle being considered exceptionally light at 39lbs., while racers were shown weighing "under 30lbs.," and one – a 51-inch—so marvellously light as 21lbs., although it must be said that these weights usually meant *minus* saddles and pedals. The double-hollow rim of the Coventry Machinists Co. was regarded as a dangerously novel innovation, and very difficult to make. The Premier bicycles were now furnished with long necks, setting a fashion which ultimately effected the abolition of the short centres hitherto used to the steering-heads. Many of the bicycles were polished so highly as to look like plated machines, plating being still regarded as a luxury attainable but by the monied few. Safety bicycles were represented by the Devon –an imitation of the Xtra and by Hall's safety, built like the Kangaroo, ultimately was, but with three cog-wheels on each side of the driving-wheel, instead of two cog-wheels and a chain.

The "Otto" was also called a safety bicycle, although its safety was always problematical; a 54-inch wheeled specimen was shown. What may be termed the monstrosity of this year was called the Ideal, consisting of a large driving-wheel surrounded by four small wheels, one in front, one behind, and two on outriggers at the sides, the idea being to prevent the rider falling in any direction. Sparrow's "Amazon" lady's bicycle was exhibited, and consisted of a machine resembling the now familiar American Star, but with the seat half way down the backbone—or front bone, lever driving, and side handles like the front handles of an open-fronted tandem, to steer the front wheel by. Tricycles were increasing and multiplying, single-driving rear-steerers being many, and the Cheylesmore introducing

THE CHEYLESMORE TRICYCLE.

us to double-driving by clutch-boxes in the ends of the crankshaft. The Humber tricycle, which had been on the road since the previous autumn, was greatly admired; and the Royal Salvo, with 46-inch drivers, was one of the nicest tricycles yet seen. Grout's "Arrow" rear-steerer, with two-speed gear, was a very promising machine, but the great weight of the bevel gear wheels, and the strain which they put upon the side tubing of the frame, soon afterwards led to their manufacture being discontinued. Meteor and Devon sociables, front steering, were exhibited, one with a canopy for India, the other with a child's seat behind, which was then a great novelty and occasioned a degree of amusement scarcely to be appreciated in these days. The Excelsior tricycle for cripples, driven by hand-levers, was brought out, and a tricycle which set the first example of very small geared-up wheels was the Rob Roy, which had an immense gun metal disc

THE ROB ROY TRICYCLE.

mounted on its crankshaft end, teeth on the inner edge of the flange gearing into the teeth of a cog-wheel on the hub of the one driving wheel. Among odd inventions was Wood's patent narrow wheel, clever in theory but hopelessly useless in practice; Lamplugh and Brown energetically started a crusade against the upholstered tricycle seat by putting on the market a leathern seat for tricycles, which ultimately gave way in process of natural evolution to the saddle for three-wheelers as for bicycles; Phillips introduced his tyre-binders (still popular), as well as a wonderful "Arguzoid" metal which has never been heard of since; and the Queen Bicycle Company sold a large number of cabinets for amateurs wishing to make their own bicycles, every part being contained in a half-finished state. A queer contrivance for luggage carrying was called the "Cassie luggage box," consisting of a metal box furnished with irons, for suspension below the front-wheel bearings,—one box on each side of the wheel. Garrood's grip pedals were designed to prevent the feet slipping,—which they did with a vengeance, wedge-shaped flanges gripping the soles of the shoes in a dangerously firm way. The Devon Sliding Spring was to allow a saddle to be shifted several inches forward or backward while in motion. Hillman's capital adjustable step (still the best on the market) was brought out, as was the Home Trainer. The chief lesson taught by this show was the inefficiency of the breaks, the manual levers of which were ridiculously short and powerless, which led *The Wheel World* and *The Cyclist* to agitate for better leverage.

For want of better accommodation, the Agricultural Hall was selected for the show of 1882, the galleries being set apart for the cycle display, whilst the ground floor was occupied by the Sportsman's Exhibition. Over a hundred exhibitors sent in all nearly seven hundred machines, it being estimated that there were quite as many tricycles as bicycles. This was the year of the "sociable craze," several first-rate patterns of side-by-side double tricycles being on the market, some arranged so that each driver drove one wheel, and a few—notably the Salvo—being balance-geared. The Phœnix sociable had its cranks arranged at cross-sections; that is to say, while one rider's cranks were in a vertical position the other's were horizontal. This should, according to theory, have aided largely in overcoming the dead-centres; but in practice it was ultimately found by experts that the best results were to be obtained by simultaneous throw. The Meteor sociable was made with a T frame, and several were bought for "club-busses," being cheap and strong; but the absence of balance-gearing told against them in the long run. The Cheylesmore Club sociable was very elegant, and fast, but had no balance-gear, and its spoon-break was very ineffective. It was at this exhibition that the first tandem was shewn, by Bayliss, Thomas and Co.; although a tandem double in which the riders sat back-to-back had been in use several years before. This and the Centaur for the first time provided

THE CENTAUR TANDEM.

machines on which both riders faced forward; but it was of the independent-chain kind, each rider driving one wheel, and the rear steering made it rather unsteady downhill. The Centaur four-in-hand was a double sociable, or double tandem—which you will,—two riders being abreast, with two behind them. The Premier sociable had the steering-handle on the extreme off-side, instead of in the middle of the machine. Single tricycles were also multiplying, the Cheylesmore being very popular. Bayliss's folding tricycle was a practical success, and the Coventry Rotary was made convertible into a sociable four-wheeler. A tricycle with driving-rods on crank-ended pedal shaft looked promising, dispensing with chains and cog-wheels; but it never achieved success. The "Dual hill-climber" was a rear steerer geared up on one side and down on the other by means of intermediate cog-wheels which were thrown in and out of action by levers. Ratchet break-holders were exhibited on several tricycles; and the tilt-rods on front-steerers of the Salvo type were being put at the side, instead of in the middle as formerly. Humber and Co. came out for the first time with a lady's tricycle, the central gearing of which was much admired; it steered the small front wheel by a spade-handle with lever in place of rack and pinion. The Merlin lever-action tricycle, working by straps on a silent ratchet-drum, was introduced; and a tricycle which deserved greater notice than it obtained was the Leicester, which may be regarded as practically the forerunner of the Cripper-pattern tricycle; it had central gearing, a low axle, and front steering, a vertical handle-post being connected to the front-fork head by means of bridle-rods; but instead of a plain handle-bar there was a rigid bar, breast high, right across in front of the saddle, and the steering-handle was a smaller bar parallel thereto, with little vertical handles for the rider's thumbs to rest around. The break was ingeniously contrived so that the rider applied it by merely resting his left elbow upon a wide lever, and to ensure the two driving wheels being equally pressed upon by the spoons, a tiny set of balance gear was interposed between the two halves of

Stanley Show, Stand 66.

£9 With Ball Bearings.

Spring Frame. Luxurious Riding.

All Machines warranted for 12 months.

GUEST & BARROW,
BIRMINGHAM.

the break-rod. Its cardinal defect was that the handle-bar prevented the rider leaning forward in the least, and was also too high to give a purchase for hill work.

THE LEICESTER FOLDING TRICYCLE.

Singer's "Velociman" was introduced practically in the exact form in which it now remains. The National differential axle—still used on the Sparkbrook tricycles—occasioned great wonderment, its action being understood by very few people. Bown showed, for the first time, his ball hubs for rear-steering tricycles; and complete sheds for housing tricycles were introduced to the public. In bicycles, a noteworthy feature was the breadth of the hollow forks used by Rucker, this maker setting an example which has been universally copied since. Mr. J. S. Whatton's racing bicycle, with handles curved round behind the rider's thighs, demonstrated that rider's idea of how to provide against injury by croppers. Ball bearings were fitted to the Facile.

THE FACILE BICYCLE.

Hydes and Wigfull showed a ball-bearing head,—made, I think, on the socket principle which is just being revived; and the usual faddist was in evidence with a pair of props to keep a bicycle upright when the rider wanted to stop. A most important era dawned in the saddle department, by Lamplugh and Brown exhibiting the long-distance saddle, dispensing with the padding which had previously been considered essential. The King of the Road lamp, too, was furnished with a wind-up burner, and an adjustable collar for bicycle axles. H. Lees came out with the Facile stop-bell; and Phillips showed a combined head-lamp and bell, the latter being mounted on the roof of the former. This exhibition was not regarded as altogether so successful as the progress of the sport and trade ought to have made it, and another change of scene became inevitable for the following year.

When it was announced that no less imposing a building than the Royal Albert Hall had been secured for the show of 1883, the prospects of cycling making strides among the upper classes were confidently prognosticated. The locality was magnificent, but the nature of the building was ill-adapted to the purpose

LOOP-FRAMED TRICYCLE.

of an exhibition. Tricycles were more than ever in evidence, the loop-framed front-steerer now supplanting the rear-steerer in popularity, although Rucker endeavoured to perfect the rear-steerer by putting a balance gear onto the crank shaft. Lloyd and Co. came out with the Quadrant tricycles, which were made rear-steering and front-steering, with racks and pinions,

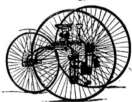

REAR-STEERING QUADRANT TRICYCLE.

on spade side-handles, and very heavy. A Premier racing tricycle, with high-built loop frame, was considered a marvel, scaling but 53 lbs. The Imperial Club was among the best-finished of the loop-framed tricycles; but to show that the rear-steerer was "not dead yet" the C. M. Co. showed a very light *racing* Cheylesmore. Bayliss and Thomas fitted adjustable handles to their tricycle, which was what few firms would do. The Omnicycle—perhaps *the* cleverest action ever invented—was reduced 40lbs. from its former weight, which had been something over 120 lbs. A "postman's" tricycle,—rear-steering, with a red-painted basket hanging behind the seat,—was spoken of as being "used extensively in the Midland postal service." The Sterling tricycle dispensed with a chain, the crankshaft cog-wheel gearing direct into the driving-wheel cog-wheel, so that the rider's feet had to revolve the cranks backwards in order to propel the machine forward. Warman showed some cleverly-designed "non-stretchable" chains. The Gnat tricycle, on the old "Dublin" plan, but with rotary chain-driving, was exhibited; and Moore's "Orbicycle" had a peculiar gearing-wheel which drove the machine at speed when treadling forward, and at power, for hill climbing, when the motion was reversed, the gears being enclosed in immense iron globes or "orbs" resembling huge cannon-balls. The first real handle-bar-steered tricycle, even more closely the forerunner of the Cripper than the previous year's Leicester had been, was the Greyhound, a light and taking little machine which unaccountably disappeared from the market very soon afterwards. The Humber tricycle

had a folding arrangement to half its handle-bar and half its axle. The Monarch rear-steering tricycle dispensed with gearing and countershaft, its rider sitting very high and working the cranked axle direct by means of stirrup pedals ; and the Otto bicycle was exhibited with a front horizontal arm carrying a castor-wheel, to make a tricycle of it. The " missing link " between tricycle and tandem was supplied by Harrington's " Krao," which resembled the modern safety *minus* its front wheel and fork, being designed to attach to any front-steering single tricycle. Singer's convertible tandem was a front-steering loop-framed single tricycle, on to the back of which a reversed loop frame was attached, making it a rear-steering tandem, the front wheel and fork being taken off. This firm showed racing machines for the first time in its history, and their " Traveller " tricycle of the Humber pattern, steered by all three wheels. An old curiosity was displayed in the shape of a " cantering propeller," a bone-shaker driven by the rider alternately raising himself and depressing his saddle as in horseback riding. The Salvo sociable was improved by being built with a tubular frame in place of the solid iron frame previously used ; and the Centaur as well as other sociables were now up to the times with balance-geared axles. " Coolie " cycles for India, made with passenger seats in front, to be driven by Coolies behind, were brought out by the Coventry Machinists Company. In bicycles, the " settled groove " was more than ever apparent, reduction of weight being the main feature. A racing Invincible scaled as low as 17lbs., but Hydes and Wigfull were still making very heavy, plated bicycles, as also was Stassen. Sparrow endeavoured to revive the glories of the back wheel break, by fitting steel rods down the backbone in lieu of a cord, and the Pilot Company sought to strengthen their breaks by lining the spoons with blocks of wood. Snelling's Antelope bicycles were brought out, and a French firm—Clement et Cie—showed a light bicycle with 200 spokes tied together by concentric wires, as well as Scuri's unicycle. Kinnaird's patent crank was the " increase of speed " fallacy of the year. An American head for the ordinary bicycle was announced as " self-steering," being exactly the hinge-jointed centres now commonly used on safeties ; and the " Ideal " or " Atlantic " bicycle

THE ATLANTIC BICYCLE.

had a second backbone and small wheel in front to prevent croppers. Warwick's hollow rims were new introductions ; Lucas had added side windows to the King of the Road lamps ; the Crypto gear first puzzled the unmechanical spectator, as did Britain's two speed gear ; some spade handles were shown with an arrangement for instantly lowering them, for hill-

climbing, by pressing a button with the knee. Bown brought out his 14 ounce racing ball-pedals, and Butler sold his rat-trap pedal-slippers for attaching to rubber-bar pedals. The Clytie bag, Lamplugh's tricycle Gladstone-bag, the " Gossamer " waterproofs, and Keat's bugles, were among the accessories, and one of the curiosities was called the Beatrice Shield, made like the folding-doors of a hansom cab, to conceal the feet of a lady tricyclist. The Bicycle Union held a meeting of exhibitors to discuss uniformity in nuts and bolts, but nothing practical came of it.

The Floral Hall, Covent Garden, was the chosen spot for the show of 1884, and continued enlargement of exhibits made the building all too small. It was a grand show, but its description is simplified by the circumstance that wholesale copying of successful patterns had now become the rule. In the previous season, the loop-framed front-steering tricycle had been all the rage, but now the Humber tricycle was

HUMBER TRICYCLE.

the pattern, and numerous close imitations were exhibited. One Humber had a tilt-rod, with a small wheel on its end, sticking out in front, to prevent croppers ; and the Lady's Humber contained, for the first time on record, a spring-fork of the now familiar pattern. A spring-framed Imperial Club was also shown, the springs being interposed between the axle-bearings and bridge of the loop-frame. The popular loop-framed tricycle had its popularity attacked by the central-geared front-steerer,—still with small

CENTRAL-GEARED TRICYCLE.

SEASON 1890.

It is a REMARKABLE FACT, but one nevertheless strictly in keeping with the INNATE PERVERSITY of HUMAN NATURE, that the MOST COMPLICATED DEVICES are frequently preferred to the SIMPLEST MEANS for attaining the same end.

To those riders who recognise the comfort of an **ANTI-VIBRATION** frame to their Safety, our

No. 5 'IVEL' SAFETY

NO. 5 IVEL SAFETY.

Affords the desideratum.   **PRICE £18.**

Do not fail to inspect this and the 15 other patterns to be exhibited by

The Ivel Cycle Co., Ltd.,

—ON—

STAND NO. 63

(Opposite the Greek Court) of the Stanley Show ; or if unable to see the Machines, send for the Illustrated Price Lists to the Company's offices,

Biggleswade, Bedfordshire.

wheel and side-handles. Two-track tricycles were rather numerous. Rucker's central-geared tricycle led the way with straight-lined **T** frame. The Devon tricycle had an extra break fitted in the shape of a hinged drag, to be pressed upon the ground by the rider's foot. The Quadrant people scored heavily with two good novelties in the shape of an expanding

THE QUADRANT STAYED TRICYCLE AXLE.

cog-wheel, for a two-speed gear, and a sociable-axle stayed by means of a number of spokes radiating from a central ring to collars at the bearing-ends. An umbrella carrier, and various luggage-carriers, were shewn on tricycles; and several two-speed gearing arrangements were contrived, each with two chains for alternate use. An attempt was made to combine the through axle with the hayfork frame of a rear-steerer; the Zephyr tricycle led the way with an elongated wheel-base; Starley and Sutton revived the Tom Tit tricycle; the Otto corrugated spokes were introduced; Bown exhibited the victor ribbon-steering which was expected to supplant the rack-and-pinion; and the Rev. J. M. Taylor personally demonstrated the action of the Oarsman tricycle which has since been revived under the name of the Roadsculler. In double tricycles, the Quadrant central-geared sociable was considered a

EARLIEST " QUADRANT " SOCIABLE.

marvel of lightness, weighing less than a hundred weight; the Europa, with a good two-speed gearing, was a very nicely designed machine; but other sociables showed but little improvement. In tandems, the Centaur Co. had a combination machine, convertible into a single tricycle, a parcel carrier, or an invalid chair. Rucker's tandem bicycle was the novelty of the year; Carver dispensed with sliding spring-tails, by using shackle-tails; the Pioneer laced wheels, with spokes headed at the hub and nippled in the rim, was well spoken of; Trigwell introduced his ball-head; Davis and Co. showed a curious backbone, split at the top to allow the halves to pass on either side of the front-wheel, thus reducing the reach. An important era in safeties was this, Hillman and Co.

THE KANGAROO SAFETY.

introducing the " Kangaroo," whilst Ellis showed the Facile upon which Adams had ridden 242½ miles in a day, and the Sun and Planet bicycle

SUN AND PLANET SAFETY BICYCLE.

was first on view. Lamplugh and Brown, and J. B. Brooks, both introduced saddles adjustable for wear, L. and B's being the Eclipse, and Brooks's the Lever Tension, whilst Harrington sold a number of clips whereby a saddle could be instantaneously detached from a spring. Lucas's lamps were improved by the fitting of an axle-bearing collar, and an appliance for carrying a little paraffin in a tube on the outside, to facilitate lighting of the lamp; Harrison sought custom for his aluminium gong; and Kelsey's ventilated handles were brought out. Goy showed two antiquated dandyhorses; Webster's aluminium was heralded as destined to revolutionize the trade; and the ill-fated Cyclists' Accident Assurance Corporation raked in the shekels of many a rider who was destined never to obtain a return therefor.

The only show of the series which can be termed a modified failure was that of 1885, the difficulty of finding suitable premises leading the promoters to adopt the novel expedient of erecting a huge marquee on a vacant plot of land on the Thames Embankment close to Blackfriar's Bridge, where the high winds

which prevailed gravely inconvenienced the exhibitors and reduced the attendance of visitors. The features of the year were the multiplication of Kangaroo-pattern safeties and the appearance of a number of rear-driving safeties with very small front wheels, the "Marvel" being one of the first made, and very tricky by reason of its extremely short wheel-base. The B.S.A. safety was one of the best of this class, and Tabor's "Antelope" was another promising specimen, which had handles of a U plan, like the front handles of a Humber tandem, so that the rider had to mount from the front. Lawson's ladies' safety introduced the drop frame now so common; but it had a very small front wheel. The Devon safety had a swing frame, giving an alternation of vertical action, forward thrust, and even backward thrust, for different gradients. The first Rover was shown, and favourably received,

THE FIRST "ROVER" SAFETY.

although it was not until the following July that the design had been so altered by the raking of the front forks as to make it a fast and popular mount. The Facile was now fitted with hollow forks, and among the curiosities of the exhibition was an ancient bone-shaker with hollow tubing all over. What was considered the most notable exhibit was Rucker's tandem safety, consisting of a Kangaroo-pattern safety with a seat, handles, and pedals for a second rider in front of its handle-bar. Rucker also showed a tandem safety formed by connecting two geared-up dwarf wheels by the same kind of bar as previously used for tall wheels on the Rucker tandem bicycle. In ordinary bicycles, the New Rapid tangent wheel made its appearance, and "took" from the first; and Travers introduced a laced wheel with butt-ended spokes. Keen's water cycle created a great sensation; it consisted of two light floats or canoes, 20 feet long, braced together parallel, with a raised saddle and handlebar in the centre, and cranks working a pair of oar-blades cleverly arranged to sweep the water, rise out, cross forward, drop in, and so sweep again in turn, two rudders connected to the handlebar by cords doing the steering. John Keen rode this machine on the Thames every day to demonstrate its practicability; but somehow it soon dropped out of the public ken. The regulation tricycle (for land) with rowing action was shown under the name of "Remicycle." A monstrosity was called "Monocycle Tetrakis," and made by framing four tall wheels together, for four riders, with a passenger seat in the centre. The "Coventry Chair" was a practical and successful introduction. Webster's Aluminium had been heralded in the press, as destined to revolutionize cycle building; but the 52-inch bicycle made with it was not favourably received, being very heavy. Tricycles with T plan frames, and also two-track tricycles, were numerous, and the "Cruiser" was

brought out to mitigate the dangers of the Humber pattern tricycle. Thresher's steering link was a means of gearing down the steering of the Humber. The Cripper tricycle made its first appearance at a show,

THE FIRST "CRIPPER" TRICYCLE.

having been brought out on the path during the previous autumn. The Coventry Rotary was shown with the saddle and pedals behind the cross tube, and bar steering, as well as in its tandem form.

THE NO. 8 QUADRANT TRICYCLE.

The No. 8 Quadrant was much admired upon making its *debut*, and the press rightly prognosticated a successful run for it. Linley, Biggs and Tandy came out with a spring frame tricycle made of twisted spring-steel rod. On the Devon tricycle, a dodge for hill-climbing consisted of a "tug," formed by fitting a handle to the footrest, by which the rider was to obtain a long forward pull when on a severe gradient. The Hansom tricycle displayed considerable originality, having a peculiar crank action with connecting-rods to a cranked axle, a cork saddle suspended on straps, spring spade-handles, and an arrangement to drive double when on a straight line, the steering-handle automatically throwing one wheel out of gear when turning. In double tricycles, Rucker's tandem-sociable was designed to combine the advantages of both machines; it was wider than a tandem, but not so wide as a sociable; the left-hand rider sat in front of the axle, and the right-hand rider behind it. Two connecting joints were shown, to connect two complete single tricycles into a tandem. The Invincible sociable stood with all the records to its credit (as, by the way, they do to this day!), and the Centaur Co. showed a tandem suitable for two ladies to ride together. The Royal Mail two-track tandem was a four-wheeler, the left small wheel being in front of the left driver, and the right-hand small wheel *behind* the right driver. The Globe Leni tandem had loop frames before and behind, and was made of springy tubes. Carrier tricycles were increasing; Bown showed a

CARRIER TRICYCLE.

two-speed gear ; the Crypto two-speed gear was combined with a balance gear in one case; and an inventive genius showed a *ten* speed gear.   In accessories, Dearlove had a cyclometer combined with a hub-lamp ; the first three-coil spring-saddle was shown by the Coventry Machinists Co.; Hawkins offered for sale a formidable "tool chest" containing cleaning and adjusting tools ; Fisher brought out the Yankee tyre-heater, the Insertus pedal-clip,—the latter a dismal failure upon advertising which much money was thrown away before it had been tried,—and the "long-distance" lamp with an immense reservoir ; an electric lamp, *only* three guineas complete, was another untested novelty ; and Crump's tricycle jacks sold well. Many of the large firms refused to exhibit at this show, which led to a reconstruction of the arrangements being mooted, the Stanley Club henceforward sharing the promotion with a committee representing the trade.

The Westminster Aquarium was the scene of the 1886 exhibition, and a greater success than ever was scored. Trick-riding by American professionals helped to attract hordes of visitors, and the exhibits were capitally displayed.   Automatic steering was all the rage, and Kangaroo-pattern bicycles vied with small front-wheeled rear drivers for popular favour, the Rover also being extensively copied. The New Rapid had by this time become a leading ordinary bicycle ; Dearlove introduced the "Rational," and Albone made his *debut*. Safeties were yet in a transition state, and one maker showed a cross between the front and rear drivers, by fitting a safety with a geared-up 30-inch driver, a small trailer, *and* a small steerer in front, the idea being that the rider could balance on the central driving wheel and steer by whichever small wheel happened to touch the ground. Bayliss and Co.'s narrow wheel sought to overcome the wide-tread objection to the safety. Starley Brothers put a spring front fork to their rear-driver. Singer showed the Courier rear driver with two chains.   The Globe Lever safety resembled the Facile, but with strap and clutch driving ; and the Sanspareil was also on the Facile plan, but with a rocking link somewhat like the Xtra. Tricycles were practically all Crippers, the front wheel being small, 22 and 24-inch wheels being spoken of as exceptionally large. The racing Quadrant, with rack-and-pinion steering on its fixed handlebar, was wonderfully light for the times, at 40 lbs. Humber put an anti-vibration spring to the front fork of the Cripper ; and the Marlboro' Club front forks had springs resembling the halves of a "cradle" spring, for the same purpose. A Premier tricycle had rack and pinion combined with moving handle-bar. Singer's Ladies' S S tricycle had its axle only 6 inches from the ground, the power being carried up to each wheel by chains, so as to facilitate mounting. The Royal Crescent was an attempt to improve away the usual fork and head, a horizontal fork moving the wheel from side to side ; and the "Radial" was a

similar idea, the front wheel having a very large open hub, with universal joint inside. A Sparkbrook tricycle, with side spade handles, dispensed with the usual rack and pinion, by its steering-rod being squeezed between two rubber rollers,—an excellent invention, but some years behind its time. Singer shewed five patterns of Carrier tricycles, which were by this time becoming extensively used by tradesmen. The Cripper pattern

CRIPPER TANDEM.

extended its influence also to tandems, nearly all shewn being of this type, although Humbers still pinned their faith to the Genuine Humber. 20 inch steerers were common, even for tandems, the largest front wheel shewn being 24 inches. The Centaur tandem, hitherto loop-framed and side-geared, was now central-geared. Carver's tandem was a four-wheeler, convertible into either Cripper or Humber type single tricycle at pleasure. The Quadrant three-wheeled tandem made its appearance, this firm's doubles having previously being four-wheeled.   Stassen showed a tandem with telescopic axle—always a hobby of his ; and the Globe tandem was shewn convertible into a passenger chair, a carrier, or a single tricycle. Few sociables were on view, the Invincible and Club being

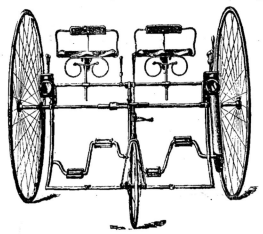

CLUB SOCIABLE.

the most perfected. Warman's one-track sociable was a great curiosity, the one large driving-wheel being placed centrally, between the riders, steered by a small front wheel, and two small tilt wheels were carried at the sides, free from the ground when the machine was running, the idea being that the riders' weight would balance on the central wheels. Bown's revolving stand of parts attracted considerable attention, and his Victor square rubbers, now so popular, were brought out. A variable-throw crank was shown by the Surrey Machinists' Co., but never came into much use. Shellard had a bearing containing only three large balls. The Abingdon chains first showed up prominently. Warman's flat rubber tyre was studded with projections, to prevent slipping.   In lamps, Barton's burner was adapted to the ordinary cycle-lamp, but burning paraffin. Lucas provided a spring-handled lamp for safeties—it having been

STAND 60.

DON'T FORGET TO SEE THEM.

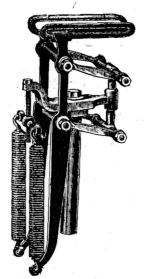

QUADRANT
SADDLE SPRING.

(PROV. PROTECTED).

Most perfect Spring ever invented.

Absolutely no Vibration.

An excellent preventive of side-slipping.

No heavier than an ordinary spring.

Adjustable to any weight from 8 to 20 stones.

Quadrant Spring Wheel.

PATENTED.

Takes all vibration from the arms and feet.

Gives increased speed with greater comfort. No drawback whatever.

PRICE LIST FREE.

The Quadrant Tricycle Co., Sheepcote St., Birmingham.

Dublin Agency: **PIM BROS., LTD., SOUTH GREAT GEORGE'S ST.**

found that lamps which kept alight on tricycles were useless on safeties,—and Salsbury devised a grip socket to keep the lamp on its bracket. Brooks brought out his Climax and Semi-racing saddles, and patent bar for quickly attaching a saddle ; Hancock essayed to sell saddles made of indiarubber; and Snell had a "saddle-tilt" to adjust the pitch of saddles. Ellis showed a neat detachable handle-bar, and the Signal Cyclometer made a good impression.

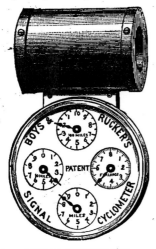

SIGNAL CYCLOMETER.

The Westminster Aquarium was again chosen, and crowded, in 1887, and the usual verdict of "the best show on record" was passed. Rear-driving safeties were the main features of the year, although tandem tricycles were in great force, the Kangaroo pattern showing evident signs of decreasing popularity. Cripper tricycles had enlarged front wheels, 26 to 30 inches being common, and in place of "automatic" or fly-to-centre steering, the stuffing-box or other stiffened steering was popular. Tricycle axles were being improved by the placing of the bearings further apart, and in many cases three or four bearings were substituted for the two bearings previously universal. The use of butt-ended spokes to wheels was increasing, and one firm showed an ordinary with spokes headed at both hub and rim, and tightened by a central joint or nipple with right-and-left-handed screws. The cross-framed safety was still deficient in bracing, in most cases. The St. George's Engineering Co. brought out a new saddle on the American plan, detachable in a moment from the ordinary bicycle ; and the Abingdon ball-head was introduced, the principle being an adaptation of Swindley's patent head, with ball bearings. The "Claviger" bicycles were also shown, for the first time, although destined never to be a commercial success. Fisher's "Non-Cropper" was a ratchet arrangement to save the rider of an ordinary bicycle from taking headers when the front wheel met an obstacle. Safeties were typified by the Ivel cross-

CROSS-FRAME SAFETY.

frame,—the first machine to demonstrate the ease with which rear-drivers could be ridden without the use of the hands,—and the Rover in its improved form.

IMPROVED ROVER SAFETY.

The rear-driving Quadrant safety, with steering as in the tricycle of the same name, was brought out. Humber and Co. were backward in the safety-race, and pinned their faith to small front wheels.

HUMBER'S FIRST SAFETY.

Non-slipping chain-adjustments were initiated by the Sparkbrook Co. The Invincible safety with single-legged forks puzzled the incognoscenti. A safety with swing-frame on the Devon tricycle principle was introduced for hill-climbing, but never achieved success. The Whippet safety appeared, with the same spring-

THE WHIPPET SPRING-FRAME SAFETY.

frame principle as had been so successful on the Whippet tricycle. Pull-up-lever breaks, with plunger spoons, were in several cases substituted for the pull-back lever breaks previously used, both on tricycles and on safeties. The Xtra was shewn on a reduced plan, its 40-inch wheel being Crypto-geared to 60 inch. The Facile, too, was now geared-up. Keating, Harrington, Dearlove, and others shewed spring forks, Pausey and Albone each exhibited a safety convertible

CROSS-FRAMED TRICYCLE,
Convertible into Cross-Framed Safety.

into a tricycle by removing the rear driving-wheel and bolting the back-fork on to a tricycle-axle with two driving-wheels. Tricycles were mostly of the Cripper class, but the Centaur Co. showed a loop-framed tricycle with the side handles brought well forward. The lady's Quadrant tricycle was introduced, with folding-over handle-bar to facilitate mounting and dismounting in front. A Premier racing tricycle weighed as little as 28½ lbs. Dearlove's "Phantom" was the first modern revival of the old Dublin pattern of tricycle, with a single rear driving-wheel, and handle-bar steering to the two front wheels. J. and H. Brookes concealed their tricycle break-rod inside the handle-bar and steering-post. Tandem tricycles were in great variety, the Humber holding its own despite the in-

HUMBER TANDEM.

crease of Cripper types, and several four-wheeled tandems being still on view. The Coventry Machinists set the fashion of connecting the ends of the handle-bars of a tandem ; they also brought out a sociable with handle-bar steering on one side. Bayliss and Thomas fitted three breaks to their tandem. Singer's successful tandem with open front, steered from the rear, made its appearance, as did the same firm's four-in-hand "Victoria" and tandem carrier for two postmen to carry letters. The Cunard tandem was convertible in such a way as to shorten the wheel-base when used as a single ; it also had a folding handle-bar in front. Trigwell's handle-bars were made with spring hinges, to check vibration. In accessories, great strides were apparent. Lucas's lamps for safeties were now provided with solid rubber handles, or brackets, to deaden vibration ; and their combination bell, and spanner with turn-screw inside it, now so favourably known, were brought out. Lamplugh and Brown's Record saddle—made of small diameter spiral springs, without any leather—was a great novelty. Fisher's spring lamp-bracket, and the "Spring Gripper" lamp-brackets, were introduced to meet the difficulty of keeping lamps alight on safeties.

The self-lubricating chain, Bown's chemical process of tyre-fixing, Otto's spring-wired tyres, the Signal

IMPROVED SIGNAL CYCLOMETER.

cyclometer, Harrison's combination gong with folding clapper, and Goy's spanner,—the handle of which formed an oil-can,—were among a vast number of novel small-goods.

The Aquarium was the home of the Show for a third time in 1888, 150 exhibitors showing about 800 machines; and the boom of the year was the war, or military, cycle, safeties, tricycles, and multicycles galore being fitted with clips for the accommodation of rifles, swords, and other warlike weapons. In ordinary bicycles, a tendency to use larger tyres and larger back-wheels was apparent, 24-inch trailing wheels being the fashion' and saddles being placed farther back than of yore, but except in minor details change there was none. An ordinary with adjustable rake was revived by the Achilles Co. Safeties of the rear-driving type had now become the leading line, cross-frames with fore and aft stays being fitted to most, while of spring-frames and spring-forks there were several very good, notably the Centaur Co.'s "Springbok" fork, Laming's hinge-jointed spring cross-frame, the Rover with spring-

BRITISH STAR SAFETY.

fork, and the British Star with a spring behind its saddle-post, the frame being hinged at the bottom angle. Band breaks, too, were put to the rear-wheels of several safeties ; and better clearance to the forks, and more strongly-secured mudguards, were very general improvements. Among peculiar safeties, the Scout had a small front and large back-wheel, something like Humber's original safety, but was driven by two chains instead of one. Several ladies' safeties were on view. The "New Rapid Safety" introduced the system of adjusting the chain by means of hingeing the lower tube of a cross-frame. The Quadrant safety

GENTLEMEN,

We have been accused of selling under price. The accusation has not come from our customers, but from our brothers in trade, prompted no doubt by jealousy.

Gentlemen, we lay the case before you—

" We " are not Manufacturers in name only.

We buy only the rough steel, tubing, rubber, and leather ; we forge or stamp all our fittings, machine them and turn them ourselves ; make our own balls, screws, nuts ; make our own chains, bearings, rims ; draw our wire ; butt our spokes ; make our own springs and saddles, and build our own machines in our own Factory, and under our own eyes.

Now, Gentlemen, do you think it is possible for us to give you a first-class article **at a reasonable price ?** because that is what we understand by selling cheap ; or the firm who must first to one man to buy his bearings, to another his saddle, to another he goes to buy his rims, and so he goes on, this machine in the end costing him 25 per cent. more than ours costs us. Gentlemen, we think we can leave the verdict in your hands.

At the

STANLEY SHOW

We shall have a few of our Machines, where we would particularly ask you to pay us a visit. We are confident that when you have seen **our samples** you will agree with us that they are, by a long way, the finest to be obtained in the market. Should you by unforeseen circumstances be unable to get up to London, we shall take pleasure in sending you our new Catalogue, and if you are too well posted to learn anything new, hand it to some wide-awake Cyclist with our compliments—to **some nineteenth century chap** who has his eyes open to a good thing, and is not too proud to learn.

GEORGE TOWNSEND & CO.,

HUNT END, near REDDITCH, ENGLAND.

WHOLESALE AGENTS FOR IRELAND:

Bowden & Sweny

26, BACHELORS' WALK, DUBLIN.

STAND 171.

was improved by its steering-rollers containing balls. Carver and others provided a two-speed gearing by the simple expedient of fitting two cog-wheels, one on each side of the driving-wheel, with different numbers of teeth, so that the gear could be altered by merely taking off the crank-wheel and turning it round to the other side of the machine. Travers introduced a break-holder on the handle-bar ; and the Premier firm tried the experiment of a raked-back steering head, giving a castor-action, with bridle-rod connection to the steering-post. The Referee and Raleigh safeties made their first appearance, as did the Lightning type of tandem-safety, the Ivel Company,

LIGHTNING TANDEM-SAFETY.

Hillman, Herbert and Cooper, and Pausey and Company, making similar machines in defiance of the patent rights claimed by Hall and Phillips. (The latter firm, by the way, have been just two years without bringing their threatened action for infringement to a head.) Pausey's tandem-safety differed from the others in having an open front, like Singer's tandem tricycle, the steering being exclusively done from the rear. Markham's Sympol tandem was a variety not resembling the Lightning type, the rear rider in this case sitting behind the back-wheel. Tricycles were fast settling into a regular groove, as ordinaries had long since done, and the Direct-steerer pattern was practically the only one shown, Humber types being almost obsolete, and the size of wheels fast approaching the "level," 30 to 36 inch drivers, with 30 inch steerers, being the general rule, and the four-bearing axle making its way. Cripper-pattern tandems were also asserting their supremacy. The Crypto Company, and another firm, turned the central-rear-driving tricycle into a tandem, the former having one pattern so framed as to be ridden by two

CRYPTO LADIES' TANDEM.

ladies, and the single machine of this make having a reducible front axle for storage convenience. The Fleetwing spring-framed tricycle was a novelty since developed. Many cross-framed tricycles were shown, the Ivel being the leader, this make being cross-

framed not only in its single form, but also as a tandem, convertible into a single tricycle, a tandem

"IVEL" CROSS-FRAMED TANDEM SAFETY.

safety, or a tandem tricycle,—four machines in one. Singer's "S S S" tricycle had a detachable stay to enable a lady to ride it, the stay fastening low down so as to help to keep the steering-post firm. The Humber tandem was improved by its backbone being extended, a larger trailing wheel fitted, and adjustable handles for the front rider.

IMPROVED HUMBER TANDEM.

The "Roadsculler" tricycle was a revival of Taylor's Oarsman ; and a wonderful machine for the Emperor of Morocco had a hansom-cab-like arrangement in front and was arranged to be driven by four slaves behind. The military element was conspicuous on Singer's stand, a "Victoria" multicycle having a very formidable appearance. Timberlake's war-cycle was like a very long-based cripper tandem, for four riders, with a Maxim gun mounted in front. Noticeable among the accessories were J. K. Starley's "Victor" wrench ; Salter's springs and spring-saddles ; White's Electrine oils; the Quadrant mud-clips ; Lucas's combination pliers, and safety lamp with steel instead of rubber links ; the Abingdon balance-gear; Townsend's

TOWNSEND'S COMBINATION PEDAL.

steel frames and combination pedal ; Bown's eccentric chain-adjustment ; Miller's adjustable-socket Bell Rock lamps ; Kelly's padlock to grip around one leg of the fork, and a spoke, of the ordinary bicycle ; and Lamplugh's saddle supported upon rubber blocks surrounded by oval-bent spiral springs. The crush this year, and consequent inconvenience under which business was transacted was so much felt that larger

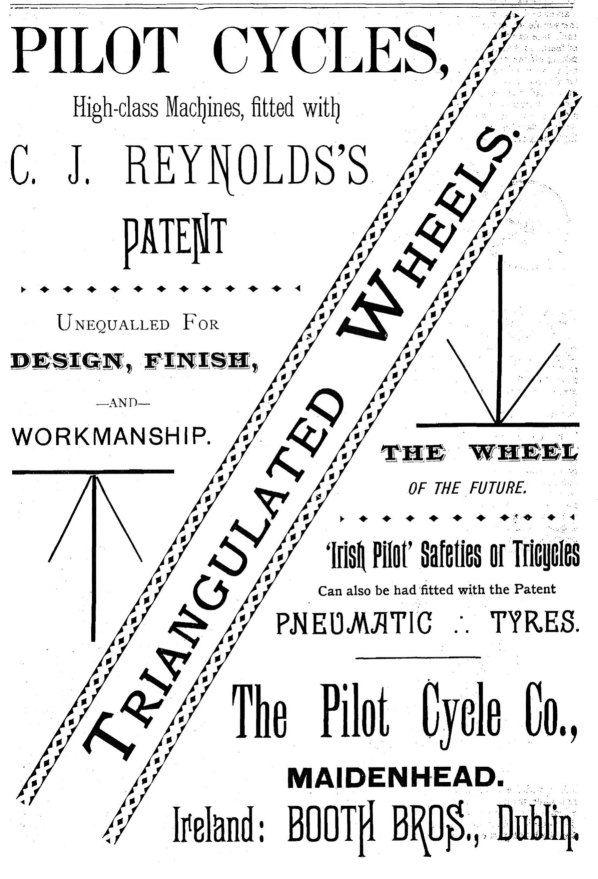

premises became absolutely necessary for the future.

An important move was made in 1889, the continually-growing demands for more space encouraging the promoters to take no less a building than the Crystal Palace, where nearly two hundred exhibitors filled the vast area and overflowed into two of the side courts, Messrs. Singer and Co., and the Rudge Company, respectively occupying one of these. The chief features were the increase of Rational ordinaries, with back-wheels from 22 to 26 inches in diameter, ball heads to ordinary and safety bicycles alike, and the total disappearance of all but handle-bar-steered tricycles. Cross-framed safeties in great numbers were usually better stayed than previously, and a growing number of diamond-framed safeties was in evidence. The great increase of cheap-class safeties was a striking feature. Spring forks and spring frames also increased,

GOLDEN ERA SPRING-FRAME SAFETY.

and breaks with shackle-spoons were very numerous. Toe-clips to pedals increased in number, and chain-adjustments were considerably improved. Some safeties with front wheels as large as 36 inches were termed "Rational" safeties, although the subsequent demand for them has not come up to expectations, their steering being defective. A great number of safeties with dropped frames, for ladies' use, gave indications of a coming "boom" in feminine bicycling, although there were some decidedly bad patterns among them. Four-bearing axles to tricycles had by this time become practically universal. The new style of sociable, resembling two safety bicycles abreast, but with only one front wheel, was shown by two firms; and another maker brought out a frame for actually connecting two complete safeties, to form one four-wheeled sociable. The Triplet tandem quadricycle, and a quadricycle for one rider, were in-

THE TRIPLET QUADRICYCLE.

troduced by Rudges. Hutchins and Hamilton's new Home Trainers, with six-foot dials for racing purposes, were a prominent feature. The Kildare safeties had driving wheels as small as 22 inches, and the Cortis bicycle was like a reversed ordinary. Numbers of tandem tricycles were shown, all on the successful "Lightning" plan. A water tricycle, constructed like two barrels for driving-wheels and a wide-dished spider wheel covered with waterproof cloth for the steerer, was the "monstrosity" of the year, although Von Lubbé's lever-driving tricycle handlebar ran it close. The Oarsman tricycle of the Rev. J. M. Taylor came out of its retirement again. Fisher exhibited a cheap stand for safeties and tricycles, forming a rest for cleaning purposes, and a French genius showed a

FISHER'S CHEAP CLEANING STAND FOR SAFETIES — ALLOWING WHEELS TO REVOLVE. PRICE 4/6.

sociable for five riders. Humber and Co., Limited, gave an indication of the immensity of their business by displaying 52 machines. Linley and Biggs created a sensation by a prize competition for the naming of their cheap rigid-framed safety. The Quadrant spring wheel was first shown. The Invincible tandem had a very attractive arrangement for the carriage of a passenger by the substitution of an upholstered seat for the front saddle. Carter's oil-tight gear case was a box designed to enclose the driving-chain in a pool of oil. Marston made his first appearance with the Sunbeam, and Buckingham and Adams made their bow as makers on their own account. Presland's electric lamp, and Haisman's revolving brush for cleaning and lubricating chains, were among the small notions. Bown showed an improved combination pedal and Keen's cranked pedal. Hook-

BOWN'S COMBINATION PEDAL.

(Rubber one side, Rat-trap the other.)

ham's wired tyres, and the machine for fixing them, were exhibited. Singer's safeties were fitted with hinged clips to lock the steering. Salter's springs, Harrison's spring-clip bells, Lucas's small and light lamp for safeties, Miller's lamp with a claw fastening to attach to the footrest or handlebar, Norris's horse-skin shoes, the Cellular clothing, and numerous other useful accessories, helped to demonstrate how thoroughly every requirement of the cyclist was provided for. Notwithstanding the distance from London of the Crystal Palace, no less than 79,360 people visited the show during the eight days. The race for the Home Trainer Championship was held, and a couple of photo-lantern exhibitions were given in a side room; and the success of the exhibition was such that the Crystal Palace is again the chosen spot for the Stanley Show of 1890.

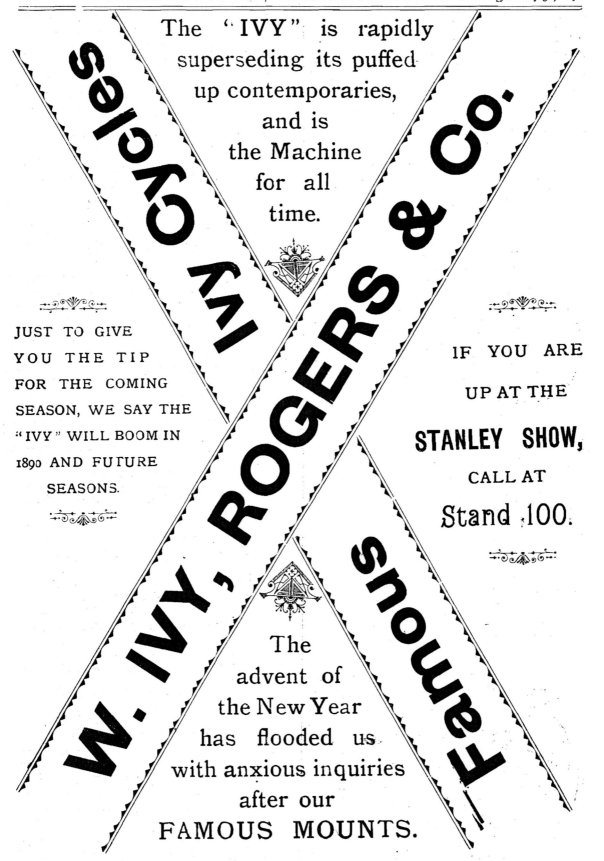

BARDS AND BIKES;

OR,

How Will Wagtale Worked His Lays.

"WAGTALE," said the editor of the I.C. & A., as he gazed benignly upon me through the bottom of a tumbler, "Wagtale, my peerless songster of the shimmering steed, the Stanley Show is upon us once again, so wake thy mews and let thy cat-calls re-echo through the pages of the I.C. & A. as in days of yore."

"Ah," I replied,
"The days of yore
Were long before
    The Jarvey came to light.
I then was free
To work for thee,
    Both morning, noon, and night."

"I know," said the editor, "that you haven't as much time on your hands as before; however, I've got an idea which I think may help you. I shall be over in England for a week or two before the show, and I intend calling on Lord Tennyson, Swinburne, and others in the poetry trade over there, and asking them to contribute something towards the show number."

"A good idea!" I cried, "but I'm afraid it will be expensive. Special poems, made to order by first-class houses, always come high."

"I think I can arrange that," returned my chief, "by offering them an 'inset' in the paper, or a free 'ad.' facing reading matter."

*   *   *

He is off, and I am alone, trying to make an epic poem on the Show. After an hour's thought, a square meal, and an interview with the office dog, I find I have evolved the following peerless stanza:—

Oh, the Stanley Show
Is the place to go,
To see the bicycles all in a row.
No man should stay
Away, I say,
Unless he has somewhere else to go.
                    Just so.

Bah! that won't do. I would be sacked without a character if I sent in such lines.

Ha! the postman's knock! Hurrah! a budget from Meeredy. Now to see what he says.

"DEAR WAGTALE.—I enclose a lot of samples of poetry, some good and some bad; select the best and touch them up a bit.

"Tennyson was a bit stand-off at first and not inclined to trade, but when I showed him how his old books would boom if advertised in the I.C. AND A., he set to work, and with pen, ink, and a few suggestions from me, knocked off a sort of jumble of blank verse and poetry. I told him it was 'spiffing!' at which he appeared pleased.

"Byron and Macaulay, I couldn't find; but a man calling himself 'Great Scott' (I presume he is the Scotch bard you asked me to look up) sent me some of his work to look over. 'The Lady of the Byke' is not bad.

"Swinburne wouldn't put pen to paper at first unless I—

"Caught him with coin from the coffers,
    Soft shimmers of silver," he said;
"Only open to opulent offers,
    And rhino rained red."

"It is not generally known that he talks in this alliterative style. He showed me a poem he was rather proud of, called 'The North Sea.' I told him to re-write it and call it 'The North Road C.,' and it would have a big sale among cyclists.

"Between you and me, he knows little or nothing about bicycles, and when I said that 'Singers' commanded big prices he thought I meant some girl called 'Patty,' who sings in comic opera! Take a poet out of his groove, and he's the most ignorant man on earth.

"I gave him something on account, and promised him a par. in The Jarvey. So crack up his goods a bit, though there's more rhyme than reason in most of them.

"He is rather given to calling a spade a spade, so look over his work carefully, or you'll have the Ladies' Club down on your laurel-wreathed nut.

"Yours en R J tically,

"R. J. M.

"P.S.—I enclose a job lot of poems which I picked up at the Poet's Exchange and Mart. 'The Exile of Erin' has a good swing, but wants to be written up to date."

———

Well, that's satisfactory so far. Now let me see what the samples are like. Yes, this poem of Campbell's is good, but would want revision—hum—hm—yes, this is better:

"THE LIERISH EMIGRANT."

There came to the Show a poor exile from Erin,
    His flask was well filled with the cold "mountain dew;"
For a cycle he sighed, but he couldn't help swearin'
    When he thought of the size of his annual screw.

"It cannot be done," cried the heart-broken stranger;
    "Eighteen from fifty leaves but forty-two.
Home I'll return a cycleless ranger,
    Without ever showing what Erin can do."

A crowd had collected by this time around him,
    So thus he continued in accents of woe,
"Oh, had I a cycle I'd quickly astound 'em,
    And show them how Ireland's champions can go.

"There never was anything grander, sublimer,
    Than the finish I made in the inter-club race,
And I'll thank ye to tell me if any hill-climber
    Can equal me either in pluck or in pace.

"Never mind who may be placed on the limit;
    Put me at scratch and I'll beat him with ease.
There isn't a bard who could worthily hymn it;
    But why am I mentioning facts such as these."

He ceased—at this moment an old maker stept in,
    And said, with an affable smile on his face,
"Will you do me the favour, dear sir, of accepting
    This cycle of mine.; 'tis the best in the place.'

"I can never repay you," the youth said.   "Be
    jabers
  With this I can easily capture the bun."
" Accounts of your wins in the bicycling papers
  Will amply repay me for what I have done."

      *   *   *

S ion home o'er the ocean the exile was steering,
  I fear in his statements the youth must have
    lied ;
For in a back yard on the green shores of Erin
  He is slowly and painfully learning to ride !

  That, I fancy, is up to date. Now, let's see what
sort of report Swinburne writes.
  Come on, Algernon ! strike the aliterative lyre.

    Oh, Palace, pellucid of crystal,
      My stars and the optic of me,
    Must I make a report—like a pistol—
      Of the wonders now wedded to thee.
    Let me grasp with a hand that's prehensile
      The notebook new bought in the Row,
    And now, having pointed my pencil,
      Commence on the Show.

    O Tempora, also O Mores,
      What wildersome wild am I in?
    Oh, dash it ! Oh, Death and Dolores,
      Now where should a poet begin?
    I would 'twere a dream of fair women
      They had asked me to sing of, for lo !
    I find a less fanciful theme in
      A Bicycle Show.

    I would sing of a mystical maiden,—
      " Faustine," or " Our Lady of Pain,"—
    My lay would be long and love-laden,
      And strike you as somewhat insane.
    Lo ! lapped in the languor of lilies.
      (Cut this, and get to the bicycles.—ED.)

    A multitude noteless of numbers,
      Like Pleades piled in a heap,
    Oh ! who has not heard of the Humbers,
      And wished they were selling them cheap.
    Good work costs you more than a penny,
      So I cannot buy one, although
    They're as good—if not better—than any
      I see at the Show.

    That peel ! 'tis a prompter's bell ringing ;
      I may as well enter and see.
    Oh, soft is the sound of the singing
      That floats from the footlights to me.
    And slap up, and sweeter, and stranger
      In here to repose,
    Than to ruefully roam as a ranger
      Of bicycle Shows.

    Oh, Lamp of our Lady Aladdin,
      What Music Hall mummer intrudes
    On the glamours that glimmer and gladden
      The doddering dulness of dudes,
    With mournful mouthings that madden
      And waggishness woeful as woe ;
    Oh, songs serving solely to sadden
      A pantomime show.

  Hallo ! this won't do ! Swinburne seems to
have strayed into the afternoon performance of
" Al.ddin " at the Crystal Palace.

  I wish I had gone over to the show myself ;
these fellows can't adapt themselves to circumstances a bit.
  Perhaps Tennyson has caught the idea better.
A Laureate ought to be able to turn out something
appropriate.
  Hum ! The start is rather unpromising.

  And so I must describe the Stanley Show,—
  I, who could never tell a Geared Facile
  From one of Salter's Springs. Well, one can learn,
  Though I am old and long way past my prime.

  Ah, me, if I had sung of modern things,
  Instead of legends of an elder day,
  Of good King Arthur, and his table round ;
  I'd now know all about the Balls o' Bown.
  And if instead of Merlin's magic wand
  I'd sing the " one big fork invincible,"
  I might disintyrate the Lamp of Snell
  From Lamplugh's Saddle and from Ulna's Bell.
  The chaos of my brain is getting worse ;
  I'll try and clear it with a snatch of verse :—

    As through the show with Faed I went,
      And listened to his sneers,
    We fell out about a bike,
    And so I told him that I'd like
      To box his blooming ears.

    Oh, curses on that falling out !
      A man in blue appears,
    And told us he'd arrest us if
      We boxed each other's ears.

    But when we came where lies the bar
      That's bossed by Mr. Spiers,
    Oh, there we waxed exceeding brave,
    And swore if any cheek he gave
      We'd box that bobby's ears.

  Here comes Mecredy, grave but garrulous ;
  And have I seen the Ivel Pony Trap,
  The Lamps of Miller, and the Lucas Lamp.
  He'll introduce me now
  To Bowden, Pim, and Carson, who, it seems,
  Are Dublin agents for the cycle trade.
  The Climax and Credenda tubes, the shoes
  Of Norris, Harrisonian Bells,
  Success and Premier and New Rapid Bikes,
  Should all be noted in my catalogue.

  Then I : " My cycling friend, you'd better stop ;
  My brain's awhirl, and if I try to-night
  To weave a legend of King Arthur's days,
  I'm sure to have Sir Launcelot bedight
  In hose of Crowe's and breeches made by White."

  Old Alfred seems to have got mixed ; well, here's
something by Lewis Caroll.   Let's see what Lewis
is carolling about.
  He evidently has got among the spring frames.

    The Whippet and the Firefly
      Where sitting in the sun ;
    They wondered if by chance the Golden
      Era had begun,
    And if the Fleetwing always flew,
      Or if it tried to run.

" Do you believe," the Whippet said,
  " The Singer knows a song,
And that the British Star can shine,
  And that it's light is strong ? "
" I doubt it," said the Firefly,
  " And yet I may be wrong."

Oh, Rover, come and roam with us ;
  We'll blow the Elland's horn ;
No Steeplechaser like the Rudge
  Has ever yet been born ;
Though some who would be faster still
  Have gone in for Cremorne.

The Weston and the Quadrant we
  Will ask to join our run ;
The Lamings too—although at school
  A laming hurt like fun.
The Victor is—well, never mind ;
  I've named them every one.

Bah ! it's no use ; none of them are capable of writing a proper poetical account of the Stanley Show. Wilson and Mecredy may write it in prose themselves.

I'll just wire to them that I'm laid up with influenza, and then go and kill myself off one of Alec's bicycles—that ensures a comfortable and unworried old age at all events.

                                WILL WAGTALE.

A "SPRING" POEM.

The flowers that bloom in the spring,
            Tra la,
  Have nothing to do with my song ;
If you fancy of flowers I sing,
            Tra la,
  Your fancy is woefully wrong.
I bleat not of bees on the wing,
            Tra la,
  Nor of nests in the hawthorn tree ;
No ink about lambkins I sling,
            Tra la,
  That playfully frisk on the lea.
I chant of the bicycle spring,
            Tra la,
  Though Hillier may say that I rave ;
Such ease to a rider they bring,
            Tra la,
  I deem them deserving a stave.

In the handles to which we must cling,
            Tra la,
  In the forks, in the saddle and wheels,
When you deaden the jar with a spring,
            Tra la,
  How much more contented one feels.
And this is the word to the world I fling,
Let us hope that vibration will die in the spring.
                                W. W.

THE "DOMICYCLE," THE WHEEL OF THE FUTURE.

AN AMERICAN INVENTION NOT ON VIEW AT THE STANLEY SHOW.

Faster than a Bicycle, Safer than a Tricycle, and Cheaper than Improved Real Estate.

ADVANTAGES OF THE "PNEUMATIC" TYRE.

Comfort

The automatic smoothing of the road before it as it were making it on the average road almost as good as riding on the path.—*Cyclist.*

Whilst the wonderful absence of vibration astonished us.—*Liverpool Athletic Times.*

I have ridden a 40-pound Safety with "Pneumatic" tyres, and it is, indeed, luxury. It runs over stones and glass and you never feel the jar.—*The Wheel.*

On setts or rough macadam, where the surface is not pitted with *deep* holes, it is no exaggeration to say that one feels no more jar than if riding on wood paving on a solid-tyred machine.—*Irish Cyclist.*

Comfort, perhaps, we may place first.—*Irish Cyclist.*

The rigid-framed Safety may be ridden roughshod with as much comfort as falls to the lot of the rider of the most luxurious "Whippet" ever built ; while, as for the combination of "Whippet" frame and "Pneumatic"-tyred wheels, the mouth waters at the very thought.—*Bicycling News.*

We found no difference in the driving and steering, and the absence of vibration was delightful. Stone setts, cobblestones, and such like roughness in the road surface, were absolutely not felt at all.—*Cyclist.*

Conservation of Power

The rider is able to accomplish greater journeys with less fatigue.—*Irish Cyclist.*

We tried a spurt down this street at 15 or 16 miles an hour, and did not feel that we were exerting nearly so much power as it would take us to drive a solid-tyred Safety over the same paving at 10 miles an hour.—*Irish Cyclist.*

The air-inflated rubber tube which forms the tyre is so elastic and, withal, so firm, that while the vibration is absorbed ere the strain can reach the framework of the machine, no loss of power is perceptible.—*Scottish Cyclist.*

Speed

And the machine seemed to slip along without any trouble at all.—*Cyclist.*

It is surprising how easily the machine moves.—*Wheel.*

Runs over rough surfaces with extreme ease, and at a pace that could not be approached on any other machine.—*Irish Cyclist.*

This made the running delightfully easy.—*Cyclist.*

Downhill, the effect of this was most marked, and the machine slid away rapidly, almost running away with us, in fact, the usual checks made to progress by the roughness of the road not being felt at all.—*Cyclist.*

Less Weight to carry

No longer need they use abnormally heavy cycles.—*Bicycling News.*

Riders will be able to use very much lighter frames without any danger of them collapsing.—*Irish Cyclist.*

Vibration, and consequently all concussion, is absorbed at the rim ere it reaches even the spokes, so that the principles which have enabled our makers to turn out sound, serviceable Roadster machines weighing 30lbs., with solid tyres, will, by its aid, enable a still further reduction, and leave its stability unaltered.—*Scottish Cyclist.*

Frames will last longer

Protected by inflated hollow rubbers, their thirty-pound roadsters will be as durable as the fifty-pounders of yore.—*Bicycling News.*

A frame so protected should wear out two frames with solid-tyred wheels.—*Irish Cyclist.*

Vibration is intercepted between the rim and the ground, and consequently the frame receives no jar except when an unusually large hole is encountered.—*Irish Cyclist.*

The tyre protects the machine.—*Irish Cyclist.*

But it enables him to ride with safety a machine from 15lbs. to 20lbs. lighter than heretofore.—*Irish Cyclist.*

Invincible on Grass

Authorities of unquestionable standing, who have watched its performances, are agreed that nothing can come near it on a grass track.—*Bicycling News.*

We feel certain that for rough grass tracks, such as we have in the North of England, there is nothing in it with the "Pneumatic."—*Liverpool Athletic Times.*

On a grass track nothing can touch it, and the rougher and softer the surface the better the machine so fitted goes in comparison to others.—*Irish Cyclist.*

A third-rate man can beat a first-rate man on rough grass if he has "Pneumatic" tyres to skim the surface with.—*Irish Cyclist.*

Racing machines must be made with "Pneumatic" tyres.—*Sport.*

On Rough Tracks or Smooth
Defies Competition

It has proved nearly as great an advantage on a hard track, such as Ball's Bridge.—*Irish Cyclist.*

In turning corners also this tyre has a very great advantage.—*Irish Cyclist.*

The "Pneumatic" had another day out on Saturday, placing two Irish championships to its credit. What it can do on grass is nothing to what it is capable of achieving on the track.—*Blue' Un.*

There were only two racing machines in use in Ireland this year, and at first they were only ridden by second and third-rate men, and yet they secured about fifty firsts, including three championships, since May.—*Irish Cyclist.*

As suitable for a fast track as for grass.—*Irish Cyclist.*

Requires little Attention

Under ordinary conditions a tyre will run for about 100 miles without being pumped, and then the process takes an incredibly short space of time—in fact, not so long as oiling the machine.—*Irish Cyclist.*

The inflation involves no "work," and is done in a couple of minutes.—*Cyclist.*

Absence of Nervous Exhaustion

That nervous exhaustion caused by excessive vibration and which tells so severely against many riders, is entirely overcome.—*Irish Cyclist.*

Anti-Vibration Contrivances Unnecessary

It has long been held to be at least theoretically correct that, if vibration is to be checked, the right place to do so is at the tyre, *i.e.,* before the vibration reaches the machine at all.—*Cyclist.*

Anti-vibration luggage and camera carriers and spring lamp brackets are quite unnecessary.—*Irish Cyclist.*

The Pneumatic Tyre and Booth's Cycle Agency,

Absence of Noise

Wearing Qualities

Complete *absence of noise* puts the finishing touch to the comfort and enjoymen of the rider.—*Irish Cyclist.*

The only point in doubt is the question of the wearing of the tyre, and from the skilful combination qualities of canvas and rubber, we are inclined to the opinion that under ordinary circumstances, with fair wear and tear, the tyre should, at least, last a season. The danger, too, of a sharp stone perforating the tube has been found be more apparent than real, the rubber being strengthened by an inside casing of canvas.—*Scottish Cyclist.*

When it is proved that the air-inflated tyres can stand as much wear and tear and knocking about as the solid rubbers, few machines will be made without them.—*Sport.*

A nail, pin or long thorn, met directly, end on, *may* penetrate, but the chance of meeting such is very remote, and even if the inner tube is cut and the air escapes, the inventor claims that the owner can be instructed to repair such a cut in a very short space of time with materials supplied for such a contingency.—*Irish Cyclist.*

Stones, or even glass, won't cut it, for they sink into the soft substance without penetrating, or glide off, or even if they cut the outside tube, the inner one will most likely escape.—*Irish Cyclist.*

Those who have used the tyre say it wears well.—*Irish Cyclist.*

Absence of Side-Slipping

Does not slip on wet greasy setts.—*Wheeling.*

It is better in ordinary wet weather by far than the ordinary Safety.—*Cyclist.*

And we believe that this "slipping bogey" is being greatly exaggerated.—*Wheeling.*

Altogether we consider it slips *far less* than the average Safety.—*Irish Cyclist.*

Under certain circumstances the "Pneumatic" slips far more than the solid tyre, and, under certain circumstances, far less.—*Irish Cyclist.*

I was able to ride the greasy setts (additionally greasy this time, by a sudden thaw having melted the mud), without experiencing any such tendency to slip down as I have felt on solid-tyredSafeties.—*Faed.*

On greasy setts it is entirely absent, and the rider can go at full pace with impunity. On hard macadam, covered with a *thin* coating of greasy mud, it slips less than the average Safety.—*Irish Cyclist.*

It shows little, if any, tendency to slip where the ordinary Safety is most at fault, *i.e.*, where stone setts and macadam are coated with a thin film of grease, such as is the case after a night's fog, or a damp, but not wet day.—*Cyclist.*

We may say we desire to correct an impression which the *Athletic News* seems to have gained from a perusal of our first article upon it, that it is a failure in wet weather. It is nothing of the kind.—*Cyclist.*

The Tricycle

Yes, experience has whetted my appetite so that I want to try it some more. I fancy that these tyres will be even more successful on tricycles than on Safeties.—*Irish Cyclist.*

For the tricycle we are inclined to think there will be a big future, for the reason that not only this side-slipping in mud is not a feature of the tricycle, but also because the machine itself requires less structural alterations than the Safety.—*Cyclist.*

Tricycles will benefit in a large degree by the *pneu* tyre.—*Scottish Cyclist.*

DISADVANTAGES OF THE "PNEUMATIC" TYRE.

Side-Slipping Occasionally

In thick, gluey mud the machine, as at present constructed, will show side slip.—*Wheeling.*

On thick, heavy, gluey mud it slips considerably, and on sloping roads it makes leeway, slipping bodily sideways.—*Irish Cyclist.*

Our further experiments confirm our deductions as to its slipping in thick mud.—*Cyclist.*

Only when the mud reaches a certain thickness and consistency does it slip, as we stated ; even then, with practice in its use, we believe this will be to a great extent got over.—*Cyclist.*

The "Pneumatic" slipped badly.—*Bicycling News.*

From experiments which we are at present engaged upon we are inclined to think that a Pneumatic-tyred tricycle is far superior as an all-round mount to any other class of machine, "Pneumatic" or otherwise.—*Irish Cyclist.*

For tricycles there is a big future before it.—*Cyclist.*

THE PRESS UNANIMOUS.

The most wonderful machine he has ever ridden. We had a trial of it yesterday for half an hour, and must add our mite o admiration to the volumes which have been showered on the "infernal machine." It is magnificent for our city streets.—*Scottish Cyclist*

With the one exception, the "Pneumatic" tyre affords the finest riding we could possibly have imagined.—*Cyclist.*

Irishmen are not very prolific of inventions, but they may console themselves by the reflection that what they do invent is worth inventing.—*Bicycling News.*

Such is the protection afforded to the frame and spokes of a cycle by the elasticity of the tyres that a new era is dawning for Irish riders and others who reside where bad roads predominate.—*Bicycling News.*

It is an Irishman, too, who bids fair, if all we are told on good authority be correct, to fairly revolutionise the trade by means of the inflated hollow rubber tyre, which has undergone a whole year's practical testing before being brought prominently forward for general adoption by the cycling public and the cycle-making trade.—*Bicycling News.*

The "Pneumatic" tyre is an assured success. It has passed the experimental stage, and achieved results on both road and path entitling it to the serious attention of the trade as well as of the amateur rider.—*Bicycling News.*

It is scarcely possible to exaggerate the importance of this invention.—*Bicycling News.*

As we have before said, it has stood the test of practical use for over a twelve-month ; and the results upon both road and path—and especially for grass racing—have exceeded even the inventor's anticipations.—*Bicycling News.*

And there seems to be no loop-hole for doubt of its complete success.—*Bicycling News.*

Enormous advantages gained.—*Bicycling News.*

We have been riding the "Pneumatic" constantly during last week, and like it better the more we ride it.—*Cyclist.*

The tyre is undoubtedly a good thing.—*Cyclist.*

65, UPPER STEPHEN STREET, DUBLIN,
AND 31, GARFIELD STREET, BELFAST.

SIGNS OF THE TIMES.

(The gaudy ensignia of past years have given
place to more sombre placards.)

Where are the signs that I loved long ago ?
Where are the colours one saw at the show ?
Funereal black, with its letters of gold,
Is all that is left of those emblems of old.

Last year as I wandered from stall unto stall,
On hues of vermilion my gaze used to fall ;
And over the I. C. AND A. stall was seen
A glorious sign-board of emerald green.

Oh, why is this change. Was it Dring who first said
"That he thought they were painting the Palace
too red ;"
And still there are some whose penurious belief
Is that colours cost very much less than gold-leaf.

WHY THE "DAILY BLOWER" HAD NO REPORT ON THE SHOW.

Which I wish to observe,
    And my reason is plain,
That for ways that are dark
    And for tricks that are vain,
Mecredy and Faed are peculiar,
    Which the same I would like to explain.

John Smith was his name,
    And I will not deny
With regard to that same
    That my statement's a lie ;
But I might be arrested for libel,
    So his real name I shall not supply.

He had come to report
    On the sights of the Show
And to write up the sport
    In a column or so.
He didn't know much about wheeling,
    But liked to appear "in the know."

Which he came to the stall
    Where O'Faed lay in wait,
Says O'Faed, " I've the call ;
    'Tis me turren to thrate."
(You observe he has learned our language)
    " Did yees iver thry Falkner tuk nate."

Now, Smith had a head
    Which could stand lemonade,
E'en the brand that 'tis said
    Ballyhooly first made ;
So he smiled and replied, " I am with you,"
    When challenged by wily O'Faed.

But he never had tried
    Such an excellent tap
As the whiskey supplied
    By this trump of a chap ;
And he said (he was getting quite sleepy)
    " On liquor like this I'd go nap."

Then he wandered away,
    Feeling glad and elate,
Though its needless to say
    That his steps weren't straight ;
And he curtly refused all assistance,
    So they left him alone to his fate.

But the notes that he made
    Were quite frightful to see,
Which can't be gainsaid,
    When I tell you that he
Talked of "two-speeded gongs with ball
        bearings—
    In order to make them run free."

Then he came to a stall
    Where the tyres they show,
Which Pneumatics they call,
    And he shouted "Hullo !
These are doubtless the snakes that are
        made by
    Delirium Tremens and Co."

So he fled from the scene,
    And was ne'er seen again,
And the "Blower" has been
    Looking out all in vain ;
But how it has lost a reporter
    Mecredy and Faed can explain.

TO THE EDITOR OF THE IRISH CYCLIST AND ATHLETE.

SIR,—I enclose a short poem, which I hope you
will think up to the standard of your Stanley Show
number.—Yours faithfully,
        HENRY W. LONGFELLOW.

Comes a marvellous invention
    From the workshops of Belfast ;
At the famous tyre's dimension
    All the makers gaze aghast.

Pity and contempt are blended
    In George Hillier's lofty stare ;
Ah, he has not comprehended
    What it is to ride on air.

Is vibration but a bogey ?
    Is it but an empty dream,
Dreamt by some enfeebled fogey
    Drifting down life's sombre stream.

We ourselves have felt the jingle,
    Felt it in each hand and limb ;
Felt the jolt and jarring mingle,
    Till the very eyes grew dim.

Now the Antelope and Raleigh
    Glide along the stony street,
Referees and Pilots dally
    With the obstacles they meet.

And men cry in exultation,
    " Here is what we all require ;
Here's the death-blow of vibration,
    Death by the ' Pneumatic' Tyre."

(Editor to Will Wagtale : "Shove this in if you want a
' fill up.' ")

THE STANLEY SHOW, 1890.

——:o:———

GREATER, grander, better, and more bewilder-ing than ever, is the thirteenth annual ex-hibition of bicycles, tricycles, and their accessories, held under the auspices of the Stanley Cycling Club and a committee of trade representa-tives, at the Crystal Palace, London. The "Show" commenced last Friday morning, and remains open until next Saturday, with no less than

TWO HUNDRED AND THIRTY-EIGHT

distinct exhibitors, some of whom display upwards of fifty machines apiece. This enormous growth in the size of the Show necessitated additional space, which has been procured by throwing open the great concert-room, as well as devoting several of the side courts to the all-pervading influence of the wheels; so that as an exhibition of only one class of goods we may fairly lay claim to Barnum's "gag," and declare this to be

THE BIGGEST SHOW ON EARTH!

Not only as to its quantity, either, is the exhibition phenomenal. On every hand is displayed an up-heaval of quality, the finish of all classes of machines being so improved that it is difficult for the onlooker to distinguish a "cheap" from a first-class cycle. Indeed, it is in the direction of low-priced machines that most improvement is manifest to the outward view, the points of construction in which the highest class of cycles excel being usually contained "in the works" not apparent to the casual glance. What is self-evident at once, however, is the increasing popu-larity of the diamond-frame and semi-diamond framed safeties, whilst there are many really excel-lent cross-framed safeties on view which are so strongly and completely stayed as to be fully as rigid as the newer designs.

BALL-SOCKET HEADS

constitute, perhaps, the chief feature of the year, the successful results attendant upon this strong and freely acting form of steering-head last season having led a great number of firms to adapt the type to their safeties, and in others the long socket-steering, without balls, is very generally relieved from liability to jambing by means of a stiff coil spring being interposed, below the socket and above the fork-top. As was anticipated, nearly every exhibi-tion has some form of

ANTI-VIBRATORY APPLIANCES,

although there are fewer radically new ideas in the direction of spring-frames than might have been expected, such tried patterns as the Whippet, the Golden Era, the British Star, and Laming's patent remaining unaltered, and the greatest variety of new designs being rather in the direction of spring-joints and spring-forks, so that an even greater number of people than might have been expected are found endeavouring to solve the mental problem of how vibration may best be annihilated, by a diligent study of one or other of the numerous safeties and tricycles which are fitted with

PNEUMATIC TYRES,

the stands of Humber and Co., Morris Wilson and Co., the St. George's Engineering Co., Man-chester Cycle Co., Snelling and Begbie, the Raleigh Co., and others, having samples of safeties or tricycles—or both—on view, provided with the large hollow rubbers which provoke much un-merited derision from the ignorant onlooker. In the universal crusade against vibration, too, Starley Brothers exhibit a safety shod with rubber tyres of a very soft description, an inch and a half in diameter; and the Quadrant Company display their spring-wheel, although, with characteristic wiliness, it is not one of the perfected pattern, but of last season's defective pattern expressly shown with all its faults for

FOREIGN MAKERS TO COPY!

Foreign makers, by the way, are represented by an Amsterdam firm,—Samuels and Co.,—with a spring back-fork-end somewhat resembling Keating's patent; while the cheery Von Lubbé comes up smiling as ever with his highly original "pump-handle" tricycle, which we are proud to say

NO ENGLISH MAKER HAS PIRATED!

Coxswain Terry, too, again shows the Amphibious tricycle, converted into a boat, in which he crossed the Straits of Dover; and the usual gentleman from a rural district sits all day upon the highly original machine, made all out of his own head, with which he is going to revolutionize the cycle trade, but explains that the sample shown is not quite so well finished as the machines he *intends* to build to order. A rather disagree-able feature of the year is the clashing of titles, the St. George's Engineering Company having their old-established name usurped by a new firm calling itself the St. George's Cycle Company, while the name of "North Road" is used by two different exhibitors—instances which, like the promis-cuous use of such names as "Antelope," which led Snelling and Begbie to relinquish their original title to the word, emphasize the need for greater use being made of the protection afforded by the

TRADE-MARKS ACT.

The Tilby-and-Marks act, by the way, takes the form of placing a cheap electric lamp for cycles on the market, although the firm's neighbours in Hackney, Nelson & Presland, have relinquished the manufacture of the one they exhibited a year ago, finding it not durable enough. Oil-burning lamps, however, are continually being improved, and one on rather unconventional lines is shewn with a double-convex lens in place of the usual glass, and a scientifically-arranged pair of reflectors claimed

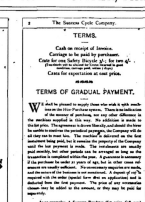

to concentrate the rays of light to an unusual degree. Such little accessories as

BREAK-HOLDERS,

too, are increasing and multiplying, and should be stocked by every cycle agent, especially in the hilly districts of Ireland. Of prepared oils, for lubricating and burning, a lively competition is apparent, and so cheaply are these many excellent preparations put up, in bottles and tins, that the cyclist has no excuse for dealing with the local oil-man and enduring the discomfort of badly-burning lamp oil, or corrosive and gummy lubricants. The "good old ordinary" is in a worse minority than ever, while

TRICYCLES

display scarcely any changes, the best types and proportions being so well recognised now that the lines are almost as definitely set as those of ordinary bicycles; most firms, too, are reducing the variety of their patterns, and now only include in their catalogues those for which the greatest demand has been experienced during the past season. There are very few tandem tricycles on view, but one

DECIDED NOVELTY

may be called either a tandem-tricycle, or a triplet-tandem-safety, being formed like the lightning tandem-safety with a third wheel and seat behind, all three riders driving the central wheel. Rudge's triplet quadricycle, in its turn, is exhibited as a quadricycle tandem for two riders only; and Humbers revive the "Krao" by fitting the rear half of a safety to the axle-bridge of any front-steering single tricycle, to convert it into a tandem quadricycle.

PNEUMATIC HANDLES

are brought out by Lamplugh and Brown, who make a barrel-shaped handle of indiarubber, with an air chamber all round. Ivory handles are put to several descriptions of the highest priced wheels, giving a decidedly tasteful aspect to the nickelled bars; and solid rubber handles are in profusion. With their usual prominence in supplying cycles to foreign potentates, the Coventry Machinists Company make a tremendous show with an immense machine, to be driven by four men, having a gorgeous hansom-cab in front for two passengers, which is built to the order of

THE EMPEROR OF MOROCCO,

a potentate whose tastes are more advanced than his love for personal exertion. Strongly in contrast to this luxurious vehicle are the highly utilitarian tricycles for use in trade, Singer and Co.'s world-renowned "Carriers" being more than ever in request; the Monarch carriers also making a brave show. The record-holding "Pilot" ordinary, with triangulated spokes, attracts as much attention as Shorland's well-worn Geared Facile; Southard's cranks are patronised by quite a large number of first-class firms; the Rovers, which "set the fashion to the world," are in strong force; whilst

FOR THE LADIES

the Whippet spring-frame is adapted to a drop-framed tricycle, and the vast numbers of ladies' safeties make us wonder where they can all go to. Among cheap and medium-classed safeties there is an increasing tendency to use rim steel instead of tubes for the frame-work The military element is not so predominant as it was two years ago; but some Premiers for the

ROYAL IRISH CONSTABULARY

are as businesslike as the safeties furnished for the various corps of Royal Marines. Luggage-carriers, gongs, spanners, saddles, and every conceivable accessory, are in profusion; and clothing especially adapted to enhance the cyclists' comfort comprises such goods as the Jaeger and Cellular systems of underclothing, ventilated hose, horse-skin shoes, knitted outer garments, and a waterproof cape, favoured by a testimonial from the Prince of Wales.

SEVERAL NEW FIRMS

bid for patronage, notably the "Claviger" people under their reconstructed conditions, and with a new name,—"Manchester Cycle Manufacturing Co.,"—whose workmanship is excellent, and the ever-growing trade of the old-established firms is an eloquent proof of the continuously advancing popularity of the sport and pastime of cycling.

THE STANLEY SHOW.
1890.

STALL-TO-STALL REPORT.

1. Credenda Seamless Steel Tube Co.—This firm holds pride of position as regards the manufacture of steel tubing. All the best makers are their customers, and they find it impossible to supply the demand. On their stall they exhibit samples of their tubing, and we inspected specimens which had been exposed to enormous pressure before bursting. In one case it took a pressure of 8 tons to the square inch, in another case 5, and in the case of a small, light gauge 4. In testing the tensile strength of a tube, it was found that it took a strain of 34 tons to pull it asunder; and in doing so the length of the tube was increased by no less than 2 inches. Last year they increased their premises so as to enable them to treble their output, and this year they have again been compelled to move into larger works, and they hope to be able now to meet the demand for their goods.

2. Brown Bros. (late of Snell & Brown, of Birmingham) exhibit a large assortment of saddles, bags, bells, lamps, chains, parts of cycles, and accessories generally. We note a very neat contrivance for cleaning a dirty chain, consisting of an arrangement for fitting two circular brushes opposite each other, and just touching the links of the chain, so that when the chain is spun the brushes remove dirt.

3. J. Salsbury.—A very neat and tasty exhibit, but so shut up under glass that we found it impossible to make a very minute examination. The well-known and world-famous Invincible lamps are there in every variety. We noticed a new pattern, very broad at the base, with an exceptionally large

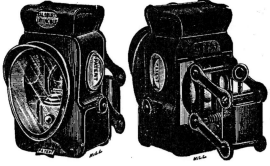

SALSBURY LAMP
(Front view).

SALSBURY LAMP
(Back view).

oil reservoir, which strikes us as being a good introduction. Mr. Salsbury's lamps possess a reputation second to none, and the fact that there is very little alteration in his standard pattern only gives proof that the lamps are as nearly as possible at perfection.

4. Perry & Co.—Hubs, pedals, ball bearings, springs, forks, balance gears, ball heads, steel safety frames, chains, and other parts, are here exhibited in great number. The firm are now supplying a very neat ball centre steering, which should meet with a ready sale. A new bottom bracket they have also invented, with a contrivance to get over the difficulty found in tightening such without overdoing it. A neat arrangement prevents the cone from turning when the nut is screwed up. This really supplies a want; for it is a very common thing for an inexperienced rider to adjust the bearings of the bracket and not notice that the tightening of the nut has also turned the cone and made the bearing too tight. Messrs. Perry's goods are all of the very highest class, and this is particularly evidenced in their hubs, which are turned out of solid steel. The ball race is right outside, and the chain wheel is in one piece. The old oil hole in the centre of the axle has been done away with, and two oil holes fitted right over the ball races—a much better arrangement. Perry's *hardened* chain is rapidly coming into favour. The wear on the rivet on most chains is very great, and to get over this the firm have fixed on a hardened bush with steel teeth, which grip firmly the side peaks. In the trade this chain possesses a very high reputation, and will, we believe, be largely used this year. The firm believe thoroughly in good stuff, and notwithstanding the high prices charged, many of the very best makers are patronising them.

5. Lintine and Co.—This firm exhibit lamps, accessories, parts of cycles, spanners, bells, enamels, churns, chain-wheels, mud-guards, &c. Their lamps are exceptionally cheap, and the "Conqueror," at 8s. 6d., struck us as being wonderful value for the money, while a small lamp called the "Richmond" sells at the extremely low price of 3s. The "Stanley" at 6s. is also a good looking article. The firm have their own brand of enamel, which they sell at 6d.—a fair sized pot, and supply a good brush with each. We noticed mud-guards made specially for Pneumatic-tyred machines, a fact which makers of this type should know.

6. H. S. Hannah.—On this stall are exhibited burning and lubricating oils, chain lubricants, nickel powder and emery powder for burnishing purposes. The feature of the oils is their extreme cheapness, a very large can being sold at the very low price of 6d. We have recently noticed it in

Look! Look!!

A GREAT

Prize

TO EVERY

PURCHASER

OF

One of our

Machines,

This takes the form of every purchaser getting the **BEST VALUE,** and a **LIFE** insurance policy against being bothered to Death **by second rate machines.**

Choose from the

'Quadrant,' 'Raleigh,' 'R. & P.,' 'Marriott and Coopers,' 'Humbers,' and the 'Wulfruna.'

Repairs promptly and correctly executed, no matter how difficult. We build Machines to your own drawings.

PIM BROS., LIMITED, SOUTH GREAT GEORGE'S STREET, DUBLIN.

N.B.—We are now Wholesale Agents for Ireland for the Quadrant Co., and we would like to hear of a few Agents wanting to make money.

Sold on the Deferred System, or large discount for Cash:—

SEWING MACHINES.

Every well-known make supplied.

TOWNEND BROS. JUVENILE CYCLES AND MAIL CARTS

All Prices, from **12s. 6d.**

NIGHTENGAL'S PATENT SPRING FORK

Fitted to any kind of Safety Bicycle or Tricycle.

☞ Those who have applied for our 1890 Cycle List, and have not received it, please send a post card; we now send it post free.

our columns, as well as the other useful preparations of this maker, who now introduces a new polish for nickel-plate, which we hope to test and report upon shortly.

7. St. George Cycling Co.—Vacant.

8. C. Lohmann.—Cycle bells and general accessories is the exhibit here; but when our representative was round there was nothing on the stall.

9. A. Churchill.—Bags, spanners, lamp oil, oil cans, &c., are here in great profusion.

10. A. Lynes & Sons.—Cycling uniforms, hats, hose, &c., and a special cloth waterproofed by a process which leaves it porous and at the same time inodorous, are here shown.

11. A. and R. Macbeth and Co.—A nice selection of safety machines, and one ordinary. The safeties are all of the same pattern—viz., semi-diamond—with a stay from seat pillar to steering post. A neatly-built socket head is fitted. The crank axle is extremely rigid. The chain tension is adjusted by sliding the hind wheel spindle in slots, and the spokes are butt-ended. A very pretty racer is made, scaling under 20lbs. The firm also build a cross-framed safety, stayed above and below, with socket steering, to all appearances a strong, serviceable machine.

12. Midland Cycling Co.—For some reason or other Wolverhampton work had formerly the reputation of being very inferior, but of late years the Wolverhampton makers have proved that though the machines may be cheap they are good and reliable, and will stand hard work. This season the advance made is very remarkable. Nowhere is it more evidenced than on the stall of this Co. The finish of the machines is really excellent, and the patterns are cleverly and scientifically designed. The greatest novelty on their stall is a spring-framed safety, which has a drop frame and is hinged just above the crank-axle. The down tube continues horizontal for a short distance, and where it rises again towards the steering post, it plays in a cylinder, the motion being regulated by a strong spring. A small guiding bar just behind the saddle prevents side play, and the action over rough ground is somewhat similar to that of the "British Star." It has also an arrangement for doing away with the vibration of the front wheel. The steering pillar is connected by ball links to the continuation of the forks, and plays freely up and down when passing over obstacles. The machine looks practicable, and the makers think very highly of it, though of course, without an actual trial, it would be very hard for us to offer a definite opinion. The firm also exhibit an ordinary cross-framed safety with this front wheel spring attachment. It is a strong, serviceable machine, well stayed both above and below. The diamond pattern "Don" safety is made with double tubes, and the chain tension is adjusted by means of a swing bracket which is extremely rigid against the tread. This machine is particularly well finished, and of very taking appearance, and although undoubtedly strong, the weight is moderate Another pattern is shown made with shell steel, with a similar swing bracket, and selling at the low price of £12. A plain cross-framed safety is also made, strongly stayed above and below, and listed at £14.

13. W. Andrews, Limited, have an exceptionally good exhibit this year. The first novelty to strike us was a convertible tricycle. It has the dropped framework, strengthened at the angle by a bracket. By loosening two nuts the main framework can be detached from the axle bridge, and the off-wheel can be detached from the axle and substituted in place of the bridge, thus turning the machine into a safety, with dropped frame suitable either for lady or gentleman. The price complete is only £24, and, in our opinion, there is a great future before this machine. We have always expressed the opinion that, taking it all round, the tricycle is much the most suitable machine for a lady, but for those who can afford it a safety would prove a great acquisition for cycling on dry roads and in country districts. Here we have a machine which can be used for both purposes, with a minimum of labour in converting it and without any extra charge, no additional parts being necessary. We recommend this machine to the careful attention of our lady readers. The firm are making special efforts to cater for agents, and, with this object in view, they have put on the market the Sanspareil Safety No 2. This machine has the popular diamond frame, but, instead of the cross-stay from saddle pillar to crank axle, it has a shorter stay nearer to the neck of the machine. The chain tension is adjusted by sliding the hind-wheel spindle in slots. The machine is listed at £16, and is really excellent value for the money. We would recommend agents looking out for a good line to examine it carefully. The Sanspareil extra strong rear-driving safety has the diamond frame, with stay from seat pillar to crank axle. In other respects it is similar to the last pattern mentioned. The ladies' safety is very neat and strong, but it is already dealt with in our description of the tricycle. The "Chapman" self-steering safety is made on the principle of the "Rothgierser" safety; but, unlike it, the saddle swings to the side the machine is turning. The frame is constructed of parallel tubes, and the saddle swings so as to influence the steering, so that the machine can be ridden quite easily without hands. A very good staunch tandem is constructed, splendidly stayed beneath and nicely finished. The firm have certainly kept up with the times, and their exhibit is a most excellent one.

14. The Bon Marche, Brixton.—Nothing but safeties figure on this stall. First, we have a strong, cross-framed roadster, well stayed above and below, and a lighter pattern of ditto. Another pattern has the semi-diamond frame, with butt-ended spokes to driver, and centre steering, and looks an excellent machine, neat and well finished—an ideal mount for a road scorcher. Another pattern is made with tangent spokes, but personally we much prefer the direct. A racer is also shown

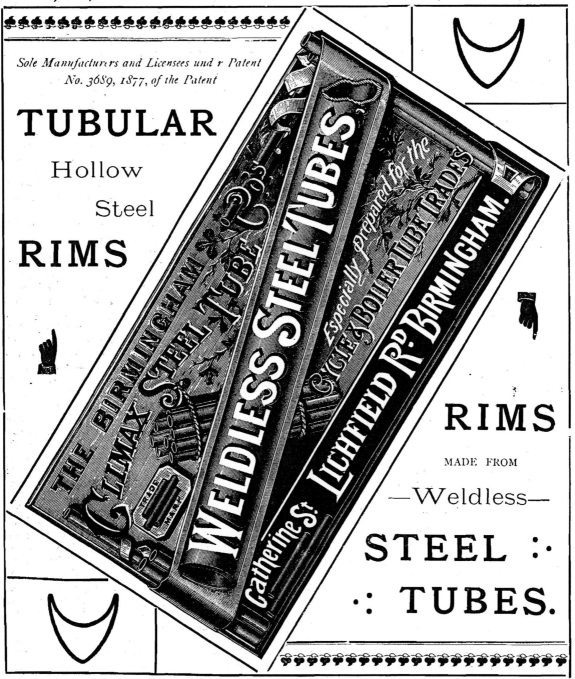

of the same pattern, scaling 17½lbs., and built to the order of Fentiman, of the Catford C.C.

15. **The Manchester Cycle Manufacturing Co.** have a large exhibit. The first machine to attract our notice was the " Irwell Pneumatic." The frame is a cross one, well stayed above and below, with neat swing bracket for adjusting the tension of the chain. We carefully tested the tread and found it rigid, and the spokes are butt-ended. It is a thoroughly good roadster in every respect, and even without being furnished with "pneumatic" tyres, would stand the hardest work. The weight complete is 48lbs., but it is only a trial machine, specially made for the show, and, when they have their dies completed and all arrangements made, the firm will be able to turn it out very much lighter. One quality which will appeal to many is the low price : complete, with "pneumatic" tyres, the cost will only be £17 10s., and as far as we know this will be the cheapest "pneumatic" safety on the market. The " Belsize " safety we have already noticed in our columns. It has an extremely powerful frame ; in fact we know of none more so. The tread is absolutely rigid, and as the crank axle bracket slides along parallel tubes at some distance apart, the danger of putting the cog wheels out of the same plane when adjusting the chain is done away with. The " Belsize " tricycle has an exactly similar frame, and possesses all the good qualities of the safety. It is light, strong, and neat in appearance. The Ladies' " Belsize " Safety is also a grandly constructed machine. In all ladies' safeties the great difficulty has been to make the backbone strong enough to bear the strain upon it, as of course, with a drop frame, it is impossible to stay them, as in the case of a gentleman's safety. The machine under notice has a backbone consisting of two parallel tubes, and the chain tension is adjusted by sliding the crank axle bracket along these tubes. The idea strikes us as very good, and we have seen no ladies' safety more calculated to stand rough roads and hard work. A neat diamond-frame safety, with cross stay, is also exhibited. It is a strong, serviceable-looking machine. The " Belsize " light roadster scales only 32lbs. We expect a large demand for the machines made by this firm in Ireland this season, for the designs of the various patterns will at once commend themselves to Irish cyclists, who are nothing if not critical ; and the firm possess an excellent reputation for the material and workmanship of their machines.

16. **West London Cycle Stores.**—The " Ormonde " No. 2 has a powerful diamond frame and cross stay, the chain adjustment is effected by means of slots in the hind forks, and the tread is rigid. A ball socket head is fitted, and the machine is turned out neatly, and nicely finished. Price complete, 12 guineas. The No. 3 has the semi-diamond frame, but a tubular stay is also fitted from top of the steering-post to the centres, which are long and powerful. A double stay is fitted forward ; the break is an excellent one, and the bearing boxes are stayed direct to the centre of rear wheel, thus giving a perfectly firm and rigid tread. It also has

a very ingenious eccentric chain adjustment. The machine looks thoroughly good throughout; in fact equal to the best. The price is 15 guineas. A cheap pattern of this make sells at 12 guineas. The Ormonde No. 1 is a plain cross-framed safety, stayed above and below with slot adjustment, and well stayed crank axle bracket, and selling at the very low price of 10 guineas. A still cheaper pattern, the No. 0 with semi-diamond frame, sells at 9 guineas. The " Ormonde " light tricycle has a quadrilateral frame with cross-stay. It is a rather unique design, and is evidently strong though very light. The rims are hollow, and balls are fitted everywhere. Price, £24. Take it altogether the exhibit is an excellent one, and does great credit to the firm. We hear the very best reports from the London district of the " Ormonde " machines, notwithstanding they are so moderate in price.

17. **The Sparkbrook Manufacturing Co.**— The safeties made by this firm are well and favourably known in Ireland. The frame has always been considered one of the best, with a tread absolutely rigid, and consequently well suited for our heavy and uphill roads. It needs no description, as it is well known to our readers. It has now been perfected by the addition of light tubes, or, in the cheaper patterns, steel wires running from the bearing cases to the neck, then forming a diamond frame with cross-stay of the most powerful description. The spokes are butt-ended, and the cog-wheels are large, a point which we have always insisted upon as being very necessary in order to ensure easy driving, for small cog-wheels undoubtedly increase the friction. A great variety of these safeties are shown of different weights, different finish, and at different prices. Some have band-breaks, and others spoon ; but all are well-finished, strong and serviceable. A new pattern safety has been introduced with semi-diamond frame, made both with and without a tubular stay running from seat pillar to neck. A neat swing bracket for chain adjustment is fitted, thus ensuring that the cog-wheels are kept in the same plane. A ladies' safety is also shown. The backbone is carefully strengthened by a bracket, and the machine is built on nice lines, with ample clearance and room for mounting. The Sparkbrook Tricycle has been altered very little, except in minor details. It has a drop frame strengthened with a bracket, and is a good, serviceable machine, well calculated to stand the roughest work. The Sparkbrook Tandem we have often noticed in our columns as being one of the strongest and most serviceable built. It is splendidly stayed from crank axle bracket to crank axle bracket, and has proved itself on the County Dublin roads a thoroughly good machine. The firm, though they have made no striking deviations from their standard patterns, have been in nowise stationary, for the improvements they have introduced are real and tangible ones.

18. **Surrey Machinists Co.** have a very large exhibit of machines, remarkable for the large tubes and rubbers which this firm have gone

GUARANTEED NO EXAGGERATION.

"THE GOLDEN ERA"

Are the most rigid and perfect anti-vibrators in the World.

AGENTS:

Dublin—BOWDEN & SWENY.
Cork—W. R. McTAGGART,
Belfast—J. SMYTH.

in for so many years. Their standard pattern safety has a cross-frame, with a stay from saddle pillar to neck, and two stays below; also stays running direct from bearing boxes to the fork ends, thus giving an absolutely rigid tread. The top stay is a tube. The weight, all on, is only about 35lbs. This safety struck us most favourably. It is absolutely correct in detail, and stayed in the strongest manner possible. The firm this year are making all their break fittings, foot rests, &c., detachable, a departure which has a good deal to recommend it. Another of their standard pattern safeties has

result which we imagine is in no small measure due to the splendid manner in which the crank axle brackets are stayed in every possible direction, as also the axle bearings and bridge. A direct steering tandem is also made, well stayed with double steering, and in which the steering can be made independent by lifting out the handle-bar pillar and inserting it in a different socket.

19. **Marriott and Cooper** have a very large exhibit of beautifully finished machines in which the structural details are most scientifically carried out. A very large number of safeties are shown.

INVINCIBLE DIAMOND FRAME.

the diamond frame, with double tubes throughout. It is absolutely rigid in every direction, and as far as construction goes we cannot possibly suggest any improvement, except that perhaps the steering post would be a little steadier if the tubes forming the upper and lower portions of the diamond were a little further apart. A ball head is fitted. The single-fork safety is still constructed; and this machine should prove especially suitable for the Pneumatic tyres, as very few structural alterations will have to be made. Mr. Smith tells us that he purposes having one fitted immediately for trial. The "Invincible" tricycle is pratically the same as last year. The open front "Invincible" tandem,

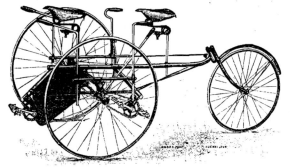

INVINCIBLE TANDEM.

on which Mr. and Mrs. Smith have done so many splendid performances, is still listed. It is a rear-steerer; but, nevertheless, the weight is so well distributed that we understand it runs steadily even down-hill. Up-hill it is unsurpassed, all admit, a

There is a cross frame well stayed above and below, a neat, serviceable machine; also a diamond frame with double tubes, exceedingly strong, and with a good rigid head. A pattern is made of shell steel. It sells at £13 10s. Their standard diamond frame safety is immensely strong; not only has it got the usual cross stay, but regular tubular forks run from the hind wheel spindle to the centre of the cross stay, the hind wheel bearings are brought out to the extremity of the forks, and the chain tension is adjusted by means of a swing bracket. On some of their machines the open link Abingdon chain, than which there is no better or more lasting on the market, is fitted. The "Ripley" tricycle is another machine with a splendid frame. It is made with double tubes throughout, and is stayed in every possible direction. The centres are long and powerful, and the machine, though so strong, is very light. A ladies' pattern is made with drop frame, and with detachable stay in case a gentleman wants to use it; the seat pillar also is small and neat, a stay running backwards, and the crank axle bracket is absolutely rigid. A rear-driving front-steering single tricycle is also shown. In tandems, the "Olympia" seems to be the only pattern now made by the firm. It is a wonderfully strong diamond frame with double tubes and a swing bracket for the chain adjustment, and we noted that the pedals were made of special soft rubber. This style of tandem is specially suitable for a lady in front, and though exceedingly light has a frame which cannot be surpassed for strength. Of course under certain circumstances there is a slight tendency for

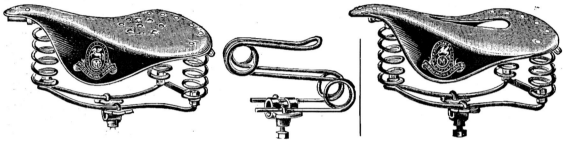
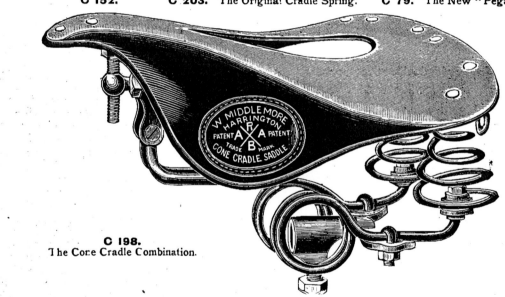
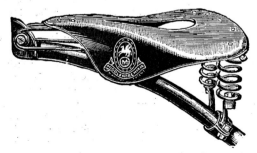
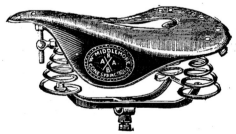

the driving wheel to slip ; but this disadvantage has been greatly exaggerated, and in actual.use we have found the machine a very fair hill climber, and ex-

LADY'S RIPLEY TRICYCLE.

ceedingly fast on the level. Another pattern is made with a detachable stay, so that it can be ridden by two ladies. The lady and gentleman who, year after year, have placidly sat on a "Humber," tandem on this stall have not only in-

"OLYMPIA" TANDEM.

vested in a new "Olympia," but have blossomed forth in a new summer rig-out, the mildness of the season no doubt deceiving them.

20. **John Barratt.**—This maker is by no means unknown to our readers. His machines, though cheap, have clearly shown that good and reliable work can be turned out at Wolverhampton. The machines are all nicely finished, even the cheapest, and built on correct lines. The "Wulfruna" No. 3 is a cross-framed safety, with centre steering and tubular stay from saddle pillar to neck, also double stays running fore and aft below. It is a neat, strong-looking machine, and is listed at the moderate price of £10. The "Wulfruna" No. 4 has the popular diamond frame, with cross stay and centre steering, feels rigid as a rock, and is neatly finished. It is really excellent value at £12 12s. The No. 5 has also the diamond frame, but of a somewhat different pattern ; socket steering is fitted, and its strength and general appear-

ance makes it quite equal, if not superior to No. 4. The price is the same. The No. 6 is a similar pattern, but more highly finished, and fitted with balls throughout. The No. 7 is a light pattern, scaling something over 30 lbs. The "Wulfruna" tricycle has the drop frame, with detachable stay from seat pillar to neck. It is a neat little machine, with a very rigid crank-axle bracket, and sells for £18. All these machines are fitted with very powerful plunger brakes.

21. **The Fleetwing Cycling Co.**—The specialty of this firm is their spring-framed tricycle. Without a block it is very difficult to describe it fully. From the bridge of the axle two powerful arms project upwards to the saddle and hold a strong coil spring, which supports the main frame of the machine. The frame is a drop one, and at the angle it is hinged to the tube which carries the crank axle bearings, and a plunger regulates the play. Not only is the vertical vibration provided for, but by an ingenious arrangement the lateral shocks which one experiences on a tricycle are minimised. A spring fork is also fitted, resembling in some respects the Humber. This machine appears to possess some excellent points, and over a rough road should be most luxurious. Dr. Richardson, who is looked upon as an authority, not only on hygiene, but also on anti-vibration cycles, rode one of these machines last year, and one of those exhibited on the stall is built to his special order. The Fleetwing spring-framed safety is also a novel machine. The frame is diamond and the rear forks slide in tubes controlled by a strong spring with a stuffing-box arrangement. From the lower angle of the diamond a hinged tube runs downward, carrying the crank axle bracket, which is strongly stayed to the centre of the rear wheel. A similar spring fork to that on the tricycle is fitted. Those who have used these machines are very loud in their praise of them, and we hope to have an opportunity of personally testing them.

22. **Pausey and Co.**—The "Pioneer" safety has a diamond frame with cross stay, ball centre steering is used, and the chain tension is adjusted by means of slots in the rear forks. The tread is firm and rigid, and strong butt-ended spokes are used for the wheels. The machine is an exceedingly nice one and is listed at a low price. The "Pioneer" tricycle has also a strong diamond frame and centre steering, the chain adjustment being effected as far as we could see by swinging the axle bridge. A two-track tandem is shown, somewhat on the lines of the Rudge quadrand-cycle. The two front wheels steer à la the old Dublin, and the frame is strong and powerfully stayed. The exhibit was evidently not complete when we visited the stall.

23. **Warman and Hazlewood.**—The Rival No. 1 is the first machine to catch the eye. It is a strong cross-framed safety, well stayed and neatly finished, and selling at the moderate price of £16 16s. The Number 3 is similar in general outline, but it is fitted with Laming's spring frame,

which we have frequently described in our columns. The "Special Rival" is a decided novelty, the frame is a semi-diamond carried rather higher than usual, and stayed from neck to crank axle bracket. The centres are long and a very efficient plunger brake is fitted. This machine is turned out in the best style and does the firm great credit. The "Rival" diamond frame is another excellent pattern. It is of the popular shape, with cross stay and is well finished throughout. The chain tension is adjusted by sliding the rear wheel spindle on the fork ends, and the crank axle bracket is absolutely rigid. It is by no means a heavy machine, and should be specially suitable for our roads. A very neat ladies' safety is shown with detachable stay in case of a gentleman using it. The "Albion" tricycle, which is the firm's leading pattern in this line, has a drop frame with strengthening bracket at the angle. The steering is central. A detachable stay runs from seat pillar to neck. It is a neat, strong machine, and is nicely finished. This firm recently received one of the largest American orders on record, being for no less than 4,000 machines, and a firm of chartered accountants have given them a certificate to the effect that out of every 600 odd machines, not more than one has been returned as faulty. We recently visited their factory at Coventry and with our own eyes saw all the various stampings and other parts being manufactured on the premises.

24. John Marston.—The "Sunbeam" safety, design A, has a plain cross frame nicely finished, but with no very special feature. The price, £13 10s., is moderate. The non-vibrating "Sunbeam" has the semi-diamond frame, which is hinged at the crank axle bracket, and a spring in compression is fitted behind the seat pillar, which absorbs most of the vibration before it can reach the rider. The front part of the frame has the forks continued to the crown piece, and the vibration causes them to sink and rise in a circular direction round the front wheel, a powerful spring regulating the movement. The contrivance appears simple and effectual. The diamond frame "Sunbeam" safety struck us as one of the nicest machines in the show. It is constructed of double tubing on the very best lines. Two parallel tubes run from the centres down to the crank axle, and thence in one piece to the centre of the hind wheel, and from the top of the centres two tubes run to the top of the saddle stalk, and thence downwards to the hind wheel, the saddle stalk binding the two sets of tubes together firmly. The chain tension is adjusted by means of an eccentric, the action of which we have previously described. The ball race is carried out to the end of the forks; butt-ended spokes are fitted to the driving wheel, and the brake is powerful. A nicer, better finished machine one could not expect to see, and it is a marvel of cheapness at the price, £16 10s., and speaks volumes for the advance in cycling construction made by Wolverhampton. The weight of this machine is only about 40lbs., and another pattern is built considerably lighter. The semi-racing "Sunbeam" safety has a semi-diamond frame,

and would be improved in our opinion by fore stays above and below. The racer is one of the lightest we have seen, and is splendidly stayed, with an extremely rigid tread notwithstanding the lightness. The "Sunbeam" tricycle is a neat machine with drop frame, without any special feature, but evidently a good sound roadster. Price complete, £22. A light pattern is made for ladies' use. The exhibit altogether reflects great credit on the firm, which has not been a very long time in the cycling trade.

25. Cycledom.—A very cheap line of machines is here exhibited, strong and reliable looking, neatly though not elaborately finished, and looking excellent value for the money. The "Cycledom" No. 1 is a cross-framed safety with stay from seat pillar to neck, at 12 guineas, and without such stay at £9 10s. The diamond frame is without the cross stay, but otherwise looks strong and reliable. It has a slot adjustment for the chain and centre steering, and the wheels are 30 inches. Price 10 guineas. The "Surrey" is a machine with a rather peculiar frame. The rear portion of it resembles the semi-diamond, except that a tubular stay runs from the top of the seat pillar to the steering post. The steering is socket, the crank axle bracket is rigid, and the adjustment is by means of slots. This looks an excellent and reliable machine, scientifically constructed, and neatly finished. Price 12 guineas. The special diamond has a cross stay and socket steering, and the weight complete is under 40lbs. A novel non-vibrating spring frame is exhibited. The rear portion of the frame is a triangle, and the backbone is hinged, as in Laming's spring frame, to one of the sides of this triangle, while a strong spring between crank axle bracket and backbone controls the play. The seat pillar is stayed to the steering post and socket steering is used. To judge by appearance this should make an efficient spring frame. One tricycle is shown, a direct steerer, with long wheel base, and a detachable stay from seat pillar to neck, at the very moderate price of 15 guineas.

26. Tilby and Marks.—This firm show a cross-framed safety with Laming's spring joint, and with the addition of a spring steering-post of their own manufacture, the pillar of the handlebar sliding in the steering post controlled by special springs at

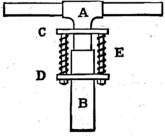

TILBY AND MARKS' SPRING HANDLE BAR.

each side. The "Harrier" No. 3 safety is a semi-diamond, strongly stayed above and below, with eccentric chain adjustment, centre steering and tangent spokes; and the No. 5 is a cross frame with slot adjustment and centre steering. It has Perry's

REMEMBER

When you visit the

STANLEY SHOW

You have not seen the latest novelties until you have
inspected our beautiful specimens of the

ORMONDE

CYCLES.

MAKERS : THE WEST LONDON CYCLE STORES,

79, Wells Street, Oxford Street, London, W.,
and 22, Holborn Viaduct, E.C.

hubs, and is a strong, serviceable machine, and appears to be very good value for the price, £8 10s.

27. F. J. Rogers.—A very nice exhibit of particularly strong machines, listed at exceedingly low prices. The "Dreadnought" No. 1 has a powerful diamond frame and centre steering, and looks up to any amount of work. It is listed at £10. The No. 2 is built on the same lines, and is listed at £8 10s. The No. 3 is of the semi-diamond pattern, but with stays above and below, a very strong combination; it also is listed at £10, and a similar pattern, but more roughly finished, is listed at £8 10s. Judging from appearance these machines are excellent value.

28. A. Burders and Co.—A large exhibit of nicely finished machines. The "Sterling" No. 1 is a diamond frame with cross stay, and is a neat-serviceable-looking machine. The No. 2 is a similar machine but lighter. The No. 3 has the diamond frame with socket steering, and is built particularly strong. The No. 4 is a cross frame with particularly well-stayed bracket. The No. 5 is a cheaper pattern, selling at £12. All these machines are built on good lines.

29. Ashton, James and Co.—A really splendid exhibit of neat, well-built machines, beautifully finished and scientifically constructed. The greatest novelty on the stall is the safety racer, which we personally saw in course of construction at Birmingham. It scales under 14 pounds, and is really a marvel. The wheel is beautifully constructed, the spokes being direct tangent. The Twin made by this firm is again exhibited. Briefly it consists of two safeties attached side by side to make a sociable. The semi-diamond frame is shown with a very novel spring fork, which runs fore and aft in a semi-circle round a portion of the circumference of the wheel, and should be both effectual and strong. These machines are fitted with a swing adjustment bracket. The "Anti-Shudder" also is a great novelty. It has an exceedingly broad rim, and two tyres are fitted of very small dimensions, and about an inch apart, the break acting on the rim between the tyres. The frame is a semi-diamond. A diamond-framed safety is also shown, which is a real beauty. It is finished in the best style, and is rigid, strong, and light. For light work a better-looking machine could not be found. A cross-framed safety is also shown, well stayed, and exceedingly strong. In tricycles a neat drop frame is exhibited, the chain tension being adjusted by revolving the bridge. A spoon brake is fitted. Altogether this exhibit made a most favourable impression upon us.

30. John Ellis and Co.—The "Rhoda" safeties sold by this firm are mostly made with curved quadrilateral frames. A new pattern is the "Sloper" safety, with semi-diamond frame, costing only ten guineas. The Langford safety is also a semi-diamond, but built exceedingly light. In the ladies' Rhoda safety, a drop frame is combined with socket steering and four axle bearings. This firm must not be confounded with Ellis and Co., Limited.

31. Tacagni, Holt and Co.—The wheels of the old racing man "Tac." are not a whit behind the times, alternative patterns being fitted with long centres or ball sockets, Southard cranks, and other modern improvements; but we regret that they were so late in arriving as to preclude our doing full justice to their merits.

32. Gadsby and Son.—The principal peculiarity here is the Lion telescopic tricycle. This is on the Dublin plan, with a single rear-driving wheel; but instead of the handle bar sloping to the front steering-axle, the steering post is vertical, and the bottom of the post is connected to the front axle by a horizontal fork. The front axle is telescopic, by a simple arrangement, requiring the removal of no nut. The Lion safety is a well put-together cross-framed machine. The

GADSBY'S LION TRICYCLE.

Lion Cripper tricycles have either two bearings or four bearings to the axles, 22 inches to 24 inches front wheels; and one of the tricycle axles is telescopic on a very original plan. A nut being loosened, the wheel is merely spun, when it automatically telescopes, the axle reducing to a width narrow enough to pass any doorway.

33. C. Cumber.—These machines are of a beautifully light class. The safeties are cross-framed, but the backbones and back-forks consist of two continuous flat tubes. The saddle post is considerably bent backward and strongly stayed to the ball socket head. A racing safety has the saddle right over the back wheel, triangular back frame, and the saddle-pillar stayed to the ball-socket head.

34. G. P. Mills.—This highly practical rider's diamond-framed safety is distinguished by a particularly strong crank bracket arrangement carrying the bearings outside the chain; and by loosening the bolts at the top and bottom joints of the diamond the triangles are shifted so as to adjust the chain. The Mills tricycle, which has such a fine stiff frame fairly tying the rear and front together, is made with an unusually narrow axle, which imparts speed whilst not interfering with stability. It is now made, too, with the top tube detachable, for a lady's use. A semi-racing tricycle is certified to weigh only 39½lbs. A beautiful light roadster ordinary, certified

30½lbs., makes us long to return to the lofty saddle, so speedy and handsome are its lines. This maker is gaining ground daily among the lovers of light and well-built wheels, and to extend his capacity for supplying the demand, a limited company is being organised with an adequate capital, with which resources the "Mills" cycles must ere long be more frequently heard of.

36. **D. G. Weston.**—This veteran maker shows the same spring-framed Cripper as last year, but considerably lighter and improved in detail. His spring-framed safety is on the same principle as the tricycle; the frame is the cross pattern, but the down tube is not fixed to the backbone, but telescopes through a socket at the cross, the strong coil spring outside the top half of the down tube providing the spring, allowing the saddle and pedals to rise and fall. The steering post has a spring resembling half a cradle spring.

37. **J. Harper & Co.**—This exhibit consists entirely of juvenile tricycles and safeties. The Tutor Crippers have a good long wheel base. The other machines are mostly of the toy variety.

38. **Bayliss, Thomas and Co.**—This old established firm have a very good show of machines of all types. The "Eureka" safety with duplex backbone, and stayed above and below, is well to the fore. It is made as a light roadster and as a full roadster at £20 and £18 respectively. Another pattern, not quite so well finished, is offered at £15. The principal novelty produced by the firm this season is the "Excelsior" safety. It has the

LADY'S EUREKA SAFETY.

popular diamond frame constructed of double tubes throughout, and with ball-socket steering. The chain tension is adjusted by means of a swing bracket, and the spokes are butt-ended. A stauncher or more serviceable mount could not be found, nor one better suited for Irish roads. We could not suggest an improvement even in the smallest detail. It is made in three patterns: full

roadster, light roadster, and the No. 1, the latter being listed at £15, and certainly it looks excellent value for the money. Butt-ended spokes are fitted, as indeed they are in all this firm's machines. The "Eureka" ladies' safety is a neat machine, with 28-inch wheels, and with a detachable stay so as to render it suitable for a gentleman. The firm exhibit some really beautiful tricycles. The "Eureka A1" quite merits the title. It has a drop frame, which is strengthened by no less than four short stays. The drivers are 30-inch, and the front wheel 28-inch. An efficient double-action band-brake is fitted. This machine we can cordially recommend, especially for ladies' use. It scales only a little over 50lbs., and a special machine at the show, built to the order of a member of the Stanley Club, turns the scale at 40lbs. The "Eureka" tandem is one of the few machines of this type that can stand the Irish roads. It is splendidly stayed, and either or both riders can steer.

39. **Townend Brothers.**—This firm is known far and wide as makers of juvenile machines. The youth's safety is a perfect little gem. It has the semi-diamond frame, and a tubular stay from seat pillar to spring post makes an immensely strong combination. The bracket is hinged and rigid as can be, and the wheels are 26 inches or 28 inches, according to order. It is built in every particular like the full sized machines, and can be ridden by youths up to sixteen years of age. Price complete, £9 2s. 6d. Another very neat cross-framed safety sells at £6 10s., and one unstayed and more roughly turned out at £3 10s. The youth's tricycle is also a neatly finished machine, but not so perfect in detail as the safety It sells at £7 10s. The firm are now making a strong diamond-framed safety for adults, which at the moderate price at which it is offered should command a ready sale.

40. **Snelling and Begbie.**—The machines exhibited by this firm are a marvel of lightness and scientific construction. They have the diamond-framed safety with socket steering, the upper and lower tubes of the frame being brought almost to a point at the steering post. The crank axle bracket is absolutely rigid to the tread, and so fine is the weight cut that the axle and cranks are made hollow. The chain tension is adjusted by sliding the rear wheel spindle on the fork ends and the chain wheel is detachable. These machines are made in the following weights:—Racer, 20lbs.; semi-racer, 25lbs.; light roadster, 32lbs.; roadster, 36lbs. A special Irish roadster is built at 40lbs. The firm also make a cross-framed safety with centre steering, and well stayed above and below, but a trifle heavier. The "Hadley" tricycle is a beautifully constructed machine. The frame is exactly similar to the safety. The steering is centre, and the chain tension is adjusted by sliding the bracket along the parallel tubes. This machine is very taking in appearance, and marvellously light. The roadster exhibited, which is to be fitted with pneumatic tyres, for the use of Mr. A. J. Wilson, weighs only a little over 30lbs.

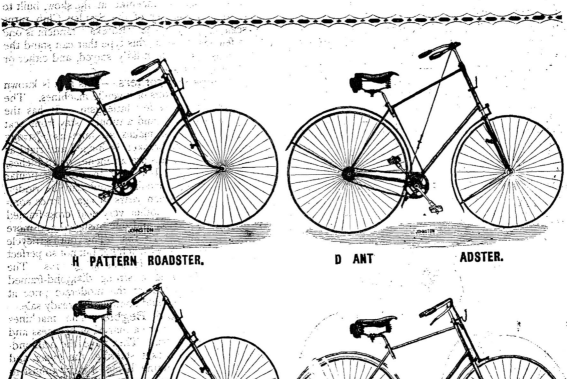

The "Hadley" tandem is an immensely strong machine, made up largely of double tubing, and stayed in every possible direction.

41. Linley and Biggs.—No alteration has been found necessary in the Whippet safety, which is shewn in both its roadster, light roadster, racer, and Continental patterns. Tricycles are of three varieties,—a Cripper pattern for the male sex, as shewn last year, a "Dublin" pattern (which was the first type of Whippet ever made), and the new ladies' tricycle, which has a curved-tube drop

THE WHIPPET SAFETY.

frame Cripper, hinged and springed on the complete system always associated with Whippets, the joints being cleverly adapted to the new type. Southard's cranks are used, Chater Lea's indiarubber chain-guard is shewn, vast numbers of the firm's pamphlet, containing "Hints on Cycling," are distributed, and an attendant is prepared to speak nearly every language under the sun. The Whippet machines head the list of spring frames, and over rough roads such as ours are not only infinitely more comfortable, but much faster than rigid frame machines.

42. St. George's Engineering Co.—We have very little to say about this exhibit, for the firm are evidently so well satisfied with the "New Rapid" machines as heretofore constructed that they have not considered it necessary to make many alterations. The No. 1 safety is almost the same as last year, except that the weight has been reduced to 47lbs. The No. 2, with direct spokes, is also similar to last year's pattern. The No. 3 is a new introduction, and one deserving of the closest attention. It has the best of diamond frames, with cross-stay. The tread is rigid, the steering central, and the chain tension is adjusted by sliding the hind spindle in the fork ends with a contrivance to prevent it slipping. In appearance the machine is a real beauty, and, all on, it scales but 39lbs., though in no particular does strength appear to have been sacrificed to lightness. This is the machine to which the firm intend fitting the pneumatic tyre, and they have one so fitted in their stall. A very pretty ladies' safety is also made with a strengthening bracket at the angle of the frame. There is ample room for mounting, and at the same time the handles are not too far away from the saddle. A detachable stay is fixed in case a gentleman should desire to ride the machine. The adjustment is similar to the last-mentioned machine,

and every little detail has been carefully attended to, as indeed is the case with all the "New Rapid" machines. The driving wheel is 28 inches. The "New Rapid" tricycle is similar in design to last year's pattern. A detachable stay has been fixed from the saddle pillar to the steering post thus increasing the strength of the frame very considerably. The weight, all on, is 60lbs., and a lighter pattern is made at 54lbs. with a short stay from the back of saddle pillar to the axle bridge. The "New Rapid" saddle and spring can be fixed to any of these machines. It weighs only three pounds and is long and flexible, like the American saddles one hears so much about. Without a moment's delay the leather can be removed, which is a very high recommendation. Another speciality of the firm is a patent clip for securing the seat pillar, by means of which seat pillars of various sizes can be used. All the machines are finished and turned out in the style for which the company have become famous, and the fact that the firm have built up an enormous Irish trade proves conclusively that their machines will stand the hardest work, for nothing defective or faulty can for long retain Irish custom.

43. Robinson and Price.—This firm adhere to the cross-frame for safeties, but use strong struts which stiffen the frame grandly. The back-wheel spindle is continued to form a real step, and the chain-flange on the back hub is readily removable, so that a new flange can be cheaply put on to the driving wheel when the teeth have got worn. The hubs are built so as to carry the ball-races far out. The neck is a very strong "centre" variety, to which both the top and bottom struts are bolted direct. A "Scorcher" safety has 35-inch front and 30-inch back wheel, with bearings in the fork-ends. Laming's patent spring is the means used for the anti vibratory R. and P. Safety. All the handlebars are curved back uniformly, not bent at an angle. Light ordinary roadsters have always been this firm's strong card, and the specimens shewn are beautifully built with grand forks and Stanley pattern ball heads. We know these machines from prolonged personal experience to be equal to the best made, and capable of bearing the hardest work on our roughest roads, and higher praise could not be given. In ease of running and comfort they are also A 1.

44. Goy, Limited.—Most noticeable among

STAND IN USE.
37 Inches long.

the machines on this stand is the Goy Sociable, on the same lines as J. K. Starley and Co.'s, two 30-

DON'T FORGET

—TO SEE—

"The Buck Jumper"

—AT THE—

Stanley Show, Stand 112.

SAMUELS & CO., AMSTERDAM.

THE 'REYNARD' CYCLES.

STANLEY SHOW, SEE STAND No. 106.

Cannot be surpassed for Materials, Workmanship, & Finish.

Every Machine guaranteed to the rider.

☞ Agents wanted where not represented. ☜

THOMAS BEARD,

LATE TOMES & BEARD,

HEATH TOWN, WOLVERHAMPTON.

inch wheels being connected by a balance-geared axle, and the riders' saddles being almost over the tops of the wheels. The steering is on the good

STAND FOLDED.
20 Inches long.

old rack-and-pinion plan, actuating a 24-inch front wheel. Goy safeties in various patterns are on view, a good detachable crank—smooth-edged and fluted—being fitted to the "Daisie." Goy's self-cleaning stand is made of wood, with metal hinges and crutches, to support a safety upside-down, and is wonderfully good value at three shillings and six-pence.

45. **Pilot Cycle Co.**—The triangulated wheel is in force here, a clever dodge to demonstrate the merits of the system being a large wheel made up with some of the spokes triangulated, and others crossed in the usual tangent style, a cramp straining the rim so that the spokes of the laced tangent showed uneven tension, while those on the triangulated principle were all evenly strained. The machines to which the triangulated wheels are fitted comprise safeties and ordinaries, the frames of the safeties being diamond, with curved-down tubes, centre-steering, and curved front forks. A pneumatic-tyred Pilot safety, with triangulated wheels, is well put together (although shown in gray paint, un-finished), with ample clearance to the wheels, and not high-priced; the total weight is 40lbs., all on, for a strong roadster. Among the ordinary bicycles, Mr. Langridge's record-holding Pilot is shown after 1,500 miles use on the road. The wheel has not been touched-up in any way, and runs true and stiff, 31½lbs. being its weight. It is an eloquent proof of the strength of these light bicycles. Ball-heads are put to the ordinaries, but the firm does not believe in balls for safeties, using hardened cen-tres instead. The Irish Pilot safety has 7-8 tyres, and scales 43lbs. The Pilots are all provided with rubbers, having a wire core, which has been peculiar to the make for no less than fifteen years,—a sure proof of excellence. The wire passes through a hole at the bottom of the rubber, so that none of the cushion is sacrificed, and so well are the tyres com-pressed on, that a 54-inch wheel has no less than two feet of extra rubber.

46. **Hathaway and Co.**—This new firm makes a good impression with some very neat-looking light safeties, cross-framed, with the saddle-pillar curved far back, and a strut connecting it to the ball-socket head, double stays fore and aft to the crank-bearings, "Referee" shaped handle-bars, and either laced tangent or direct spokes.

47. **S. Griffiths and Son.**—Both safeties and tricycles of this firm display marked improvement in finish. The "Clyde" safeties are shown with both cross-frames and diamond-frames, with centre-steering; and a Clyde, with cross-frame supple-mented by a strut from saddle-pillar to steering-post, has a long socket-head with coil springs above and below the socket. The "No. 1 Universal" is a strong-looking cross-framed safety, with seven-eighths corrugated rubber. These safeties vary from ten to fifteen pounds. The Clyde tricycle is a good-looking Cripper pattern, with 28-inch steerer and 34-inch drivers, a drop frame with attachable stay, long axle with four Bown bearings, swing adjust-ment to the crank bracket, and not to be con-sidered at all dear at £18.

48. **Fletcher Cycle Co.**—This firm's recent novel advertisement attracted considerable atten-tion to their stand, where another advertising novelty was found in the shape of an offer to take orders, during the show only, for their £13 10s. safety at £7 10s. each. The "Godiva" safety, which constitutes the prize for the guessing compe-tition, is a cross-framed safety of strong appearance, with a rim-steel forestay and sliding adjustment to the crank-bracket. For Ireland, a special pattern is called the "Erin-Go-Bragh!" with a stiff cross-frame, long centre steering, well-fitted mudguards, a mudguard over the chain, tubular front stay, curved front fork, and square rubber pedals. The Gem safety, at £17 10s., is a diamond-framed light roadster, with vertical strut, and a well-designed centre neck. The Ivanhoe safety combines the half-diamond back frame with half-cross front. A well-worn cross-framed safety with a large basket on its handlebar was labelled as having been ridden by a commercial traveller weighing 12 stones, and carrying 40 to 70 lbs. of samples, some astonishing number of miles.

49. **J. B. Ford & Co.**—Among the safeties here, a double curved-tube quadrilateral frame was noticeable, with a particularly good eccentric chain adjustment, contained in the angle of the back forks. A cross-framed safety with outside bearings had a queer arrangement called a com-pound crank, which was supposed to give increased power; but this we regard as a fallacy, the only practical effect of the arrangement being to con-siderably widen the tread. Some cross-framed and diamond-framed safeties seem remarkably good value at £9 10s. each; and a very good juvenile safety at £5, and a tricycle 10s. more, completed a compact exhibit.

50. **G. L. Morris, Wilson and Co.**—The Referee safeties, which have been so extensively copied by many other makers, are here found in all their native purity. As racers, and light roadsters, there is nothing better than the Referee, and those which have been brought to Ireland have stood our roads in an astonishing manner. The pattern has been found so good that no alteration is apparent except in small details, a great many of which, however, display the same care and ingenuity which led the Referee to achieve its existent success. The ball socket head, so fre-quently imitated, is improved by being made rain-tight. The back-fork chain adjustment is remo-

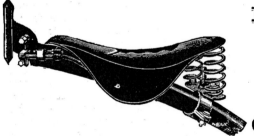
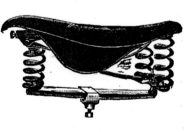

delled, so that it now acts both ways to true a wheel's tracking. The tangent spokes are headed through the hub-flanges and pipe-nutted at the rims. Perhaps the most noticeable machine on the stand is a Referee light roadster safety with pneumatic tyres, built for our Mr. A. J. Wilson, which has every imaginable improvement, and would be termed "about thirty-two pounds" according to the usual "makers' weight," but which we saw weighed on the official scales, complete with detachable mudguards, square rubber pedals, footrests, and brake, the weight being 40lbs. exactly. The brake is an original idea, the usual spoon being replaced by a long roller of small diameter, which the makers think will act better than a spoon on the hollow tyre. The Referee tricycle has a frame very similar to that of the safety, the rear parts of the diamond being flat tubes placed endwise on to the line of strain.

51. **Bettman and Co.**—Chief among novelties in the popular "Triumph" cycles is a tricycle with 28-inch wheels, readily convertible into a safety by removing but three screws, and shifting the chain, the left driving wheel of the tricycle having a chain-flange on its hub, so as to serve as the driving-wheel of the safety. The general features of the Triumph frame have been so recently described in our columns that they must be familiar to our readers. Strength of design is very evident, and the Irish pattern is well adapted to the requirements of our roads, and, from personal trial, we can speak as to its easy running and "life." A new type is the Triumph tandem-safety, built under licence from the "Lightning" patentees, convertible into a single safety. Light roadsters are built on the same lines as the full roadsters, but of lighter guage, and a very neat racer also follows the firm's regular shape. Cranked-out cranks are fitted to all machines, preventing the ankles striking against the edges.

52. **Herbert Smith & Co.**—Laming's patent spring frame, as applied to so many makes of safeties, was here shown in its new form, adapted to a semi diamond frame, the joint being neat and strong. The stand upon which this was mounted consisted of a wooden trough, à la "Starley's wheel-washer," with brushes and rollers to readily cleanse the rim of a wheel from dirt.

53. **L. Von Lubbe** again shows his old tricycle fitted with a jointed handlebar, the right half of which can be pumped up and down, working a crank on the hub of the front wheel.

54. **W. Fisher & Co.** exhibit their combined cleaning stand and home trainer, upon which any tricycle or safety can be suspended by the fork-ends, and used for stationary indoor practice, the cost being but 14s. 6d., or with a friction roller to increase the resistance, five shillings extra.

55. **H. Edwards.**—This Welsh maker again shows the Mona Safety,—a tall Rational ordinary with a lever action very similar to that of the "Claviger" tall bicycles.

56. **G. Cousins** comes out with a curious safety, having a 30-inch back wheel and 18-inch front, a drop-frame constructed of solid square

steel, of springy nature, and with a front fork very similar to Bown's "Victor" spring fork. Instead of the usual saddle, a broad leathern seat with back-rest is provided, something like Lamplugh's leathern tricycle seat. The machine shown was stated to be the first made, and was only roughly finished.

57. **Osmond & Co.**—This is a new firm, the head of which is younger brother to F. J. Osmond, the amateur champion. He shows two safeties and a racing ordinary. The former is a neat-looking diamond-framed safety with ball-socket head and a good form of eccentric chain adjustment. The tall machine is a very handsome racer, with ball head and Humber style of details. Osmond's heel-clips for pedals are a great novelty, and extremely simple, consisting of a piece of steel rod three inches long, projecting from one of the pedal plates in such a way as to rest in the angle of the shoe-heel, taking the place of toe-clips. They can be put to either rat-trap or rubber pedals, and cost only half-a crown a pair.

58. **G. & P. Hookham** show samples of their spring-wired tyre, which is too well known to need a description, and also a safety built with Hookham's patent suspension head, in which the socket of a curved diamond-framed safety is suspended by an external spring from the rigid inner post.

59. **W. H. Halliwell** displays the "Brighton" cross-framed safety with stiff stays all over; a straight front fork, 30 and 32-inch wheels, and screw to prevent the back wheel spindle slipping in the fork ends, all for £9. The "Electric" safety has a diamond frame, with curved central strut and other details as the other, for £12. Here is also seen a perambulator with an automatic brake to prevent its running away when unattended.

60. **Quadrant Tricycle Company**—So satisfied with their patterns (the oldest types in existence) are "the Quadrant people," that no new machines are on view, a fine display being, nevertheless, made with the perfected patterns of the No. 8 Quadrant, No. 15 tandem, and No. 17 safety. Even the No. 8 A—built to satisfy the demand for a small-wheeled tricycle—has had a twelvemonth's experience on the road, although absent from last year's show. *The* novelty of the year is the new saddle spring, the action of which is purely vertical; and, unlike any other spring, it is in tension, not compression. Having no lateral play, it imparts great steadiness to a safety, and reduces the tendency to side slip, while its spring can be adjusted to any degree of elasticity, to suit various weights and tastes, by the simple adjustment of a nut. The spring-wheel safety shown is not of the perfected pattern, but it is purposely exhibited in its original faulty form so that foreign buyers will not copy the improved springs. One of the No. 8 tricycles is shown with the company's camera-carrier combined with a snug little railed seat, for the convenience of a child, the vertical spring being a source of unprecedented luxury for juvenile passengers. The types and merits of the Quadrants are too well known to need dilating upon, the tandem in particular being

a unique touring machine, most admirably suited to Irish roads, with immense brake-power, and a really remarkable hill-climbing and luggage-carrying capacity. Boyd's double-action spoon brake is shown on a No. 17 safety. This is particularly good for very hilly country. The ordinary spoon brake is connected by a double shackle to a reversed spoon behind the fork-top, so that the friction of the wheel on the one spoon draws forward the second spoon, which then adds its power to retarding the wheel.

61. **Cooper, Kitchen and Co.**—The "Elland" spring-framed safety is here the chief novelty, and very thoroughly are the anti-vibratory appliances carried out. The frame generally is of a diamond pattern, but instead of rigidity we find flexibility everywhere. Between the top of the front fork and the steering post half a "cradle" spring is interposed; and the mudguard is tubular, its lower end being firmly attached to a horizontal fork made of spring steel. A similar combination of spring-steel fork and curled wire springs is provided for the rear wheel, the curled spring being placed behind the saddle-pillar. This combination dispenses with all working joints, and all this without introducing any flexibility between the working parts, the handles, saddle, and pedals being rigid as regards each other. A very long ball-socket head is fitted to this, as also to the rigid safeties; the chain-adjustment, too, is new and good, the tubular back-fork ends terminating in screws passing through a female-threaded socket on the back-wheel spindle, with nuts each side for adjustment. Cross-framed safeties are shown in the same pattern as last year, having been found satisfactory, and the leading line is the diamond-frame, whether spring or rigid, the long ball-socket head being a good feature. Cheap safeties are shown at £9 for cross-frames, and £12 for strutted diamond frames, and tricycle patterns display no alteration from those of 1889. A pretty safety for a juvenile is made with double diamond frame, constructed of rim-steel, with ball bearings all over except pedals, at £8. The "Collina" toe-clips are exceedingly light, and suitable for either rat-trap or rubber pedals, costing only 2s. per pair.

62. **Howe Machine Co.**—This old-established company's most noticeable exhibit is a tandem-tricycle, with a single rear driving wheel, and unusually long base, the front rider being behind the cross-bar which carries the two side steering-wheels. The ends of the U plan front handlebar are stiffened by stays, which drop to the end of the cross-bar, and the whole design is very promising, the placing of the load further back than is usual on this type of tandem tending to increase the bite of the driving-wheel. Other tricycles shown are of the Cripper pattern, both single and tandem, a single being also shown on the same lines as the tandem before described. Safeties of the fashionable strutted-diamond pattern have long ball-socket heads and rim-steel struts, and other safeties of the cross-frame type are variously priced to suit all pockets. General ordinaries have "rational" points, and a racer is well designed.

63. **Ivel Cycle Co.**—Better than ever are the Ivels, a year's experience having brought about great advances in the machines made at Biggleswade. The cross-framed Ivel safety, which did so much to popularize its type, is now stayed between the neck and the saddle-pillar, as well as below; and the diamond-framed Ivel has a curved down-tube. Curved front-forks are used on some patterns, but the original straight fork is still recommended. A half-diamond framed safety is also stayed from neck to saddle-pillar, and the Lady's Ivel safety, which was the forerunner of modern ladies' safeties, is on view. The Ivel tricycles are mainly on the familiar cross-framed pattern, and the tandem tricycles, which still hold the 24 hours road record, have been found so satisfactory that the pattern is retained. A ladies' tricycle has drop frame and detachable stay; and all the tricycles have the powerful swing crank-bracket, peculiar to this firm. Ordinary bicycles, too, are again made, Dan Albone's first successes having been with the tall wheel; and the present patterns are fully up to the times. The general finish of all the Ivels is vastly improved, and bids fair to bring these excellent wheels into renewed favour in Ireland.

64. **Coventry Machinists Co., Limited.**—The most imposing machine in the whole show is—as usual with this firm—an immense coolie-cycle, built for the Sultan of Morocco. The front part consists of the body of a hansom cab, splendidly upholstered, but with a 28-inch steering wheel in front instead of a horse. The driving mechanism is behind the cab, being four wheels of 44-inch diameter, framed together in a way resembling two sociables, four saddles being provided for coolies to occupy, driving the machine forward, and the front pair steering. The whole framework and spokes are plated, and the handles are of ivory, the body of the cab being painted green and gold. Being intended for use in a district where the roads are very flat, the driving of this will not be so hard as might be imagined. In more commonplace exhibits the company is strong, the model A "Swift" having Keating's spring-forks adapted to the rear as well as the front wheel, the arrangement being remarkably simple, and calculated to still further enhance the already-great popularity of this safety in Ireland. On another Swift safety, a handlebar shown hinged to the steering post in such a way that the whole bar has a vertical motion, a spring, interposed some three inches behind the hinge, controlling this play and of course intercepting such vibration as would otherwise reach the handles. Ball socket steering is found here, too; and a particularly good line seems to be the "Model C. Swift," at £15 10s., with balls everywhere. A new departure in tricycles is the Swing-frame tricycle, built with an open curved-down frame, the diagonal part of which—in the line between the axle-bridge and the front wheel—is not rigidly attached to the bridge, but is loosely mounted parallel to another diagonal down-tube carrying the cranks, with a spring to steady it, so that the saddle, handlebar, and front wheel can shift or roll from side to

side, without affecting the driving-wheel or pedals, enabling the tricyclist to lean over in turning corners, and similarly enabling either driving-wheel to rise over an obstacle without throwing the rider out of an upright pose. A tandem safety is made with an open front, for a lady, **U** plan handlebars being substituted for a cross handle bar. Needless to say, all the machines on this stand are finished in the beautiful style for which this firm has been so long noted.

65. Centaur Cycle Co. — Here we have another firm whose name is a household word in Ireland; and so recently have we described the 1890 patterns of Centaurs in THE IRISH CYCLIST AND ATHLETE, that a repetition of the details is unnecessary. Suffice it that the firm's reputation for originality in design and strength of construction is fully maintained. The Centaur D.S. tandem deserves especial notice, by virtue of its being the legitimate development of the first front-steering tandem tricycle ever built; in its present form it can be ridden by either sex on either seat. While this tandem carries us back in fancy to the years gone by, the " B.S. Diamond " safety typifies the very latest development, the ball-socket head showing that with all their originality the Centaur Co. are not above adopting a good thing when they see it. The band break on the rear wheel of the Sharpshooter safety is one of the few effective rear-wheel breaks in the show. Among the single tricycles, the " Centaur D. S. No. 4 " particularly struck our fancy, the frame being a strong design well tied together to resist fore-and-aft strains. Nearly all the current patterns of Centaurs are made with special modifications to meet the requirements of Irishmen, the firm having gone into the matter very thoroughly, even to the extent of issuing a special Irish catalogue showing the machines which they recommend for use in our country.

66. Guest and Barrow.—The British Star spring-framed safety is now too well known to need much comment. The designs this year are but slightly altered; and the oval front tyre introduced last season has been found so successful that the firm purpose extending the use of it; it is wired to prevent its twisting in the rim, and gives considerably more relief from vibration than a circular rubber would. The "Concertina" spring between the saddle post and back-fork-top is retained unaltered, no instance being on record of its giving way; and from prolonged personal experience we can vouch for its thorough efficacy in reducing vibration and its great speed and comfort on rough roads. A lighter pattern is now introduced, as well as a cheaper grade with the same kind of front fork as is used on the "Girder." The latter-named machine is cunningly devised to provide a very strong frame at less expense than usual, a novel system of construction being applied to it whereby most of the parts are bolted together instead of brazed, the angles being scientifically designed to resist all strains. It is a wonderful machine at £9, and for juveniles it is made so strong as to bear practically any weight, the makers very rightly considering that boys usually give a machine rougher usage than do grown-up persons.

67. Thomson and James show a solitary specimen of the " Mohawk " safety, which has a frame formed of two triangles, and a curved down-tube, the curve of the tube being the reverse way to the front of the driving wheel which it crosses.

68. Crypto Cycle Co.—These conscientiously good makers have considerably lightened their patterns for 1890, and a most noteworthy machine is the Princess tandem, driven by a single rear wheel and steered by two side wheels à la Blood's patent. With its new five-sided back-frame, breaks to all three wheels, and convertible into a single tricycle, it yet weighs only 69lbs., or in full roadster form, compressible so as to pass a narrow doorway, under ninety pounds. The Agilis tricycle is now made with a five-sided diamond frame, and also in form for ladies' use. These tricycles are thoroughly well made, and suited for the Irish market, the tandem being the nicest type to our taste, while it is better up and down hill than is generally supposed. We have been riding one continually for some months, and can speak of it in the highest terms. The company's new Crypto safety has a good five-sided frame, very long ball-socket head, and is really cheap at sixteen guineas. The Crypto cyclometers are well known, and now made in two varieties,—the usual long-distance recorder and a " Daily Register " form, the latter recording up to 100 miles, and being capable of having its dial set back to zero at any moment.

69. J. K. Starley and Co.—" The Rover has set the fashion to the world," and J. K. Starley and Co. are the makers of the Rover, of which they may well be proud when they look around them and see how universally the trade has followed the lead set by the Rover, which made its first appearance at the "Wheeleries" on the Thames Embankment. Here, in 1890, the good old Rovers raise their honoured steering-heads in proud beauty, the frames being modified to suit every taste, the " Popular," " Universal " and curved quadrilateral frames being now supplemented by a handsome diamond-frame, vertically strutted of course. A new patent handlebar is made of a piece of flat spring-steel,—a very simple and effective form of anti-vibration;—and the grand old big-front wheeled Rover with straight fork is also on view. The modernized sociable exhibited last year is improved in many respects. The driving-wheels are connected by a balance-geared axle with a foot-break in the middle, and both riders enjoy a perfectly open front, the single-steering wheel (actuated by a spade handle and a rack-and-pinion) being carried on the forward end of a **T** frame. A ladies' Rover with the wheel and chain covered in by strings is beautifully got up with extra plated parts and ivory handles. We are pleased to see our old friend the Coventry Chair in an improved form, with central-geared cranks and considerably lightened all round. A Rover tricycle—Cripper pattern—has the spring front fork which was put to the safeties last year, supplemented by ball links to keep the joints steady although free.

70. **Starley Bros**.—This ranks as one of the best exhibits in the show. The first machine to catch our eye was the "King of Diamonds," a diamond frame, as the name implies, with firm tread, long centre steering and butt-ended spokes. Another pattern is fitted with socket steering, and the weight all on is under 40lbs. The "Psycho" light roadster is on the same lines and scales 30 lbs., while the semi-racer is somewhat lighter. The "Black Diamond" is an excellent introduction. It also has the diamond frame and is constructed throughout of shell steel. It is rigid and strong and really nicely finished, and sells at the moderate price of £14 10s. This machine should suit the pockets of many of our readers, and from a careful examination and thorough knowledge of the work turned out by this firm, we feel sure it will stand the severest tests. The ladies' "Psycho" cycle is one of the prettiest safeties on the market. The frame is dropped with a graceful curve and the weight is well under 40lbs. A semi-diamond framed safety is made with well stayed bracket and centre steering, and scaling under 40lbs. It is a handsome machine and looks strong. The "Psycho" safety full roadster has the diamond frame and is a strong machine, fit for any amount of knocking about on the Irish roads. The "Psycho" tricycle has been altered slightly in detail, the frame instead of going to an angle being curved gracefully downwards and upwards. We have ridden one of these machines for three seasons and can testify in the strongest manner to its running and wearing qualities, and except for a trifling repair it never cost us a penny though subjected to hard usage. We never mounted a better, and in hill climbing especially its superiority was most marked. A special light pattern is introduced this season for ladies' use. It is even a prettier machine than the other, being constructed on the most graceful lines, and it weighs, all on, under 40lbs. For our roads we would not recommend any but the very lightest riders to try this machine, though with pneumatic tyres it would be strong enough for the heaviest. Another safety, facetiously styled the "Rheumatic," is also exhibited with $1\frac{1}{2}$ hollow tyres made to resemble the pneumatic. Though we have not dilated at length upon the exhibit, it is not because it is not equal to the best, but the firm have not gone in for a multiplicity of patterns and have no startling novelties. What they have got is good and practical, and they have enough patterns to satisfy the tastes and suit the pockets of all buyers.

71. **J. Devey and Co**.—A modest, but highly meritorious, show of the low-priced cycles for which the name of Devey has long been proverbial, includes the No. 1 and 3 safeties, for which Bowden and Sweny, the Dublin agents, tell us there has been such a strong demand last season. Both are remodelled for 1890, and while the cross-framed No. 1 remained at £10, the diamond-framed No. 3 is reduced to £12 ; a healthy sign at a time when prices generally are on the rise, and it would be impossible to find a better quality of safety at the price. The No. 2 is a variation of the No. 1, similar in all details except the rubbers, which are of full

inch diameter for Irish roads, and increase the cost to £11. The "Northern X" ladies' safety is perhaps the cheapest safety for a lady upon which any reliance can be placed ; and another machine catering for the fair sex at a moderate price is the Northern X tandem tricycle, with 34-inch drivers, 28-inch steerer, drop frame in front, and detachable stay—complete for £22. A 52-inch rational ordinary is called the Judge, and has a very big back wheel and cowhorned handle-bar ; listed at ten guineas.

72. **Sharratt and Lisle**.—This is another firm of low-priced celebrity, rejoicing in the name of "Star" for their wheels, which go as low in price as £8 10s. for a cross-framed safety with cone bearings, centre steering, plated, enamelled, and gold-lined, surely an attractive mount for those of shallow pockets. A similar machine, but with ball-bearings, costs £11 ; and for £13 10s. a diamond-framed safety is put in, with balls everywhere, patent chain-adjustment, and the enamel lined gold and grey, giving a very pleasing effect. A rational ordinary is also staged, with long cranks, extra raked front fork, 22-inch back-wheel, and balls all over (including pedals), for £11. A large number of these machines were sold in Ireland last season, and gave the greatest satisfaction ; in fact they were far better than many high-priced machines. We can thoroughly recommend them.

73. **Ellis and Co**.—The Geared Facile is one of the few safeties which have been found so perfect as to need no alteration ; here are seen some of the beautifully light—yet strong withal—bicycles which showed up so well when ridden against time last year, notably the one upon which Shorland beat the record from London to Edinburgh, and won the Wanderers' hundred miles road race near Dublin. In addition to this, and the standard pattern of that speedy ordinary, the Farringdon, quite a collection of novelties are on view, most noticeable being a rear-driving chain safety without a handle-bar, the steering handles being placed in the usual position but mounted on the top ends of tubes which drop in a straight line to the front wheel spindle, the appearance from the front being therefore that of a **V**. The head is close above the front wheel rubber, and a cross tube midway up the **V** connects the handle tubes to the steering head. This makes a very steady front wheel, and gives a rigid pull to the handles. Another rear-driving safety is on the "Geared Facile" plan of driving, but with reversed levers and wheels of regulation size. The "Facile" tricycle is a central rear driver with Facile lever action, and open front ; and it is made so that by removing the two front wheels with their cross-bar a bicycle wheel can be substituted, the machine being thus converted into a rear-driving Facile-action safety suitable for a lady's use. Yet another variation of the firm's build is the "Facile" carrier tricycle, driven in the same way as the other rear-driving Faciles, but with a roomy box mounted on springs on its front frame. The "Facile" safety (which, by the way, is considered the best machine made, by experts such as Gerald Stoney and R. E. Brenan) requires to be well known

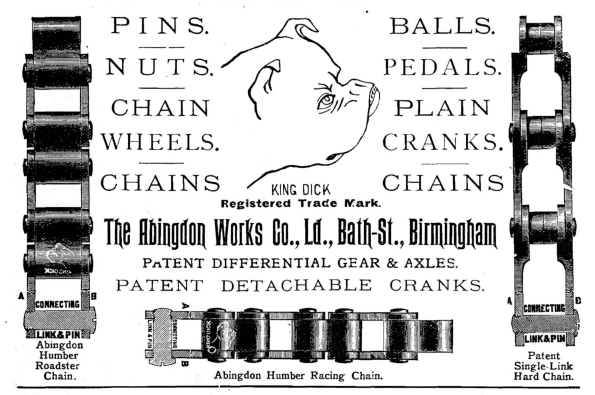

to be thoroughly appreciated, and a short trial is never satisfactory. Last season they gained a firm footing in Ireland, and we expect to see a run on them this season. As regards wearing qualities, lack of side-slipping, safety, and comfort, no machine could be more suited for Irish roads. The Sympol tandem safety is also shown on this stand ; it is a much shorter tandem than others, as the rear rider sits right over, or slightly behind the top of the rear-driving wheel, instead of both riders being between the wheels ; and while the front rider's cranks are geared to the rear wheel in the usual way, the rear crank shaft passes freely through the hub of the rear wheel, and a chain conveys the power from it to the front crank shaft, whence it is returned to the driving hub.

74. Calcott Brothers and West.—This firm pin their faith to safeties and tricycles of recognised patterns, free from any peculiarity, such as they know will find a ready market. The "XL" safeties are consequently of the usual cross, diamond, and semi-diamond framed varieties, at prices varying from twelve to twenty guineas, the latter including ball head.

75. The Goulden Syndicate.—The "Golden Era" is *not* a spring-framed machine, but a perfectly rigid-framed machine with anti-vibratory appliances. That is how the makers put it, at least, and they ought to know. So well-known is the Golden Era principle that a description is scarcely necessary ; in brief, the anti-vibratory appliances consist of telescopic saddle pillar and steering post with very long springs inside affording a wide range of play ; and the type has been well tested during successive seasons. The fact that the firm's exhibit was labelled with the announcement that "a large quantity of these machines have been built to the order of Messrs. Bowden and Sweny, sole agents for Dublin," indicates that the demand for "Golden Eras" in Ireland is very firm. It is not only to safeties, however, that the Golden Era principle is applied, tricycle frames adapting themselves readily to the system ; and even on a Rational Ordinary the patent insulators are successfully applied to the back fork with such effect that no saddle spring is considered necessary. Mr. Goulden is certainly with us heart and soul in our contention that anti-vibration appliances do not appeal *only* to "the aged, the nervous, and the infirm," and he recounts a number of instances in which the adoption of his machine materially increased a man's pace and enabled him to outpace men who were much faster previously.

76. Humber & Co.—This firm have the largest and best-arranged exhibit in the show, and in the short space at our disposal it will be utterly impossible to do justice to the very many types and patterns they display. The No. 2 safety is their standard this year. It has the diamond frame with cross-stay and socket steering. The driver is 28 inches, steerer 30, and a splendid new swing bracket is fitted for the adjustment of the chain. For rigidity and strength, and at the same time extreme simplicity, we see nothing to beat this bracket in the show. The

veriest novice can manipulate it without danger of the chain wheels getting out of the same plane. This machine is built as a light roadster at 39lbs. weight, and with pneumatic tyres and band brake, all on, it is 48lbs., though the firm are prepared to build a Pneumatic safety which will stand the roughest roads at 38lbs. weight. The No. 3 safety has a similar frame with sliding chain adjustment like last year. The No. 4 is the same as last year, with a patent anti-vibrator and sliding adjustment. The racer also is much the same as last year, but it has been very considerably lightened, and now scales complete 21lbs. Messrs. Humber and Company have always been against the indiscriminate reduction of weight, and any machine they turn out may be relied upon to stand really hard work. A road racer is made 27lbs., and a roadster, with mudguards and all complete, at 33lbs. The No. 7 safety has a patent self-steering head, the centres are in advance of the lines of forks and at a different angle, thus turning the front wheel into a castor. The ladies' safety is a beautiful mount ; the chain and rear wheel are completely covered, and the chain tension is regulated by means of the firm's swing bracket. In every detail the machine is complete, and though strong it scales well under 40lbs. There is ample clearance for mounting, and at the same time the handles are not too far forward. We can recommend this to our lady readers. No. 11 and No. 12 are juveniles, and splendid value at the money. No. 13 is a diamond-frame almost identical with No. 2, with 30-inch wheels, and selling at 16 guineas. The 13A is similar in design, but with centre steering, and sells at 14 guineas. Both these machines are exceptional value, and, we believe, can be had fitted with pneumatic tyres. The No. 14 is a safety with semi-diamond frame and centre steering, and sells at £14. All their safeties are complete in detail and beautifully finished, and whether made at Beeston, Coventry, or Wolverhampton, the workmanship and material can be thoroughly relied upon, for in this respect no firm in the trade has a better reputation than Humber and Company. In tricycles, the No. 1 gents' is the best. It has been altered somewhat this year, and the frame now is a diamond with socket steering and patent anti-vibrator. We consider this machine has been greatly improved by the change, and it is now as perfect as a tricycle well can be. The drivers are 30 inches and the steerer 24 inches ; but they can be built to order with 36-inch drivers and 26-inch steerer. The No. 3 is a ladies' tricycle with drop frame, and in appearance is very similar to the gents', with the exception of the absence of the upper stay. A detachable stay, however, is supplied in case a gentleman should require to ride the machine. The dress guards are particularly good, there being no possible place where the dress can catch or get soiled. This machine can be fitted with pneumatic tyres to order. The No. 4 is a light pattern of the No. 1, scaling, all on, 48lbs. It has a spoon brake instead of the band, except in case it should be ordered with pneumatic tyres.

The No. 5 is a ladies' tricycle, and is almost identical with No. 3, except that it is very much lighter. Pneumatic tyres will be fitted to this machine to order. The No. 6 is a racer. It is similar to last year's, except that the weight has been slightly reduced. The No. 4 is a gentleman's tricycle selling at £21, and the No. 8 is a ladies' tricycle, similar in design to No. 5, but selling at £21. This machine can be fitted with pneumatic tyres to order. A beautiful juvenile "Cripper" sells at £7, and other patterns are from £3 15s. to 10 guineas. A very great novelty of the exhibit is the No. 13 tandem attachment. This consists of the rear portion of a safety which, by the manipulation of one nut, can be fixed to any tricycle, thus turning it into a complete tandem with three driving wheels. The machine has been very fully tested and runs beautifully. The firm purpose making this attachment, so that it can also be used for a single safety, and when this change is completed the demand for the combination machine should be very great. All Beeston Humber machines are dear to purchase, but economical in the end, for the owner's repair bill is sure to be small, and they fetch a splendid price second-hand. We speak from experience. Our last season's Humber cost us 6d. for repairs.

77. Hillman, Herbert and Cooper.—One of the largest and most perfect exhibits comprising every type and pattern of machine, many of them already well and favourably known in Ireland. The "New Model A" safety is a staunch roadster, with diamond frame, with cross-stay and ball socket steering, or plain, if so ordered; the spokes are butted, and a good sliding adjustment bracket is fitted. This is a machine we can thoroughly recommend for Irish roads, for a nicer or stronger design could not be found. The "Model B" is somewhat similar, but with centre steering. The "Model C" is the machine ridden by Holbein in his marvellous record rides. It has semi-diamond frame, with a fore-stay, and also a stay from seat-pillar to neck. A swing bracket is fitted, and the machine is built throughout as lightly as possible, consistent with strength. The "Model E" has a plain cross-frame, and sells at £10 10s. od. It is excellent value, and those in search of a cheap but reliable mount should not pass it. The "Model F" is a diamond-frame safety, constructed of shell steel, fitted together in a way which gives it the appearance of a tubular frame divided vertically, except for a few inches at the neck. It has centre steering, a swing bracket, and butted spokes, and is neat in appearance, and of undoubted strength. The price is £12 12s. od. Military safeties are also shown, and a neat ladies' with 28-inch driver. In tricycles the No. 1 is a good staunch roadster, with dropped frame and band-brake. The open link chain is used, and is adjusted by means of a sliding bracket. The drivers are 36-inch, and steerer 28-inch; but another pattern somewhat lighter is built with 30-inch drivers, and a curved dropped frame, instead of being brought to an angle at the crankaxle bracket. Of the two the last-mentioned is the

neatest, and it is specially suitable for a lady. A second grade tricycle is offered at £18, and is certainly grand value, for except in finish and minor details it is equal to the No. 1. The No. 3 Light Roadster has also the dropped frame, but with a strengthening bracket at the angle. An excellent tandem tricycle is shown, very strongly stayed, and a good machine, too, as we know from the experience of cycling friends. A well-stayed tandem safety is shown, and a variety of juvenile machines.

78. Success Cycle Co.—Noted as they have always been for great strength and honest construction, the Success cycles are now vastly lightened, without sacrificing the splendid principles identified with the pattern. A very light roadster Success shews the arched crank bracket in its original form with the exception that the bearings are contained (with a universal joint) in a rigid case at the angles of the back-fork tubes and the arch bracket, the chain being adjusted by tuning-fork ends, and a very nice arrangement to get true adjustment and prevent the lock nuts slipping, consists of a milled-nut which has forward as well as backward action in the place of the end nut so common on such contrivances. This type is also shown adapted to pneumatic tyres. The neck is very strong and light. The Ladies Success Safety has a curved-down frame, retaining the arch-bracket. The brakes on these machines are fitted with an open ring at they fork-top so that they can be instantaneous detached. In the Irish Success roadster, ⅞ tyres are used, and extra care is bestowed upon all such little points as the fitting of the mudguards, butt-ended spokes being used on all these machines, with an extra thick guage to the Irish pattern. A capital arrangement of connecting rods is shown, to convert any two Success safeties into a sociable quadricycle, the steering being made differential, and unusual care being taken to arrange the fastenings of the cross bars so that they will be rigid. This conversion necessitates no alteration whatever in the safeties themselves. Since this firm made its *debut*, the unvarying good quality of their machines has justified their name, and the "Success" is continually becoming more popular in Ireland and Scotland especially.

79. Joseph Bates.—Prominent among the exhibits here, is a safety with a knuckle-joint spring action just like Laming's patent, but with the important difference that the spring is invisible, being concealed in the knuckle-joint itself. It is fitted to a semi-diamond frame. Another feature here is Harper's patent combination tyre, which consists of an ordinary rubber tyre covered outside by a semi-circular band, so that there is only a small strip of rubber bare, each side, between the edges of the rim and the outer band; the idea is presumably to save the tyre from being cut,—a microscopical advantage scarcely compensating for the obvious disadvantages of a metal rim.

80. Perry, Richards and Co.—Here we have another firm which is a credit to Wolverhampton, their safeties being mostly of the "Referee" type, and finished in a style far different to what used to be typical of "Wolverhampton work." A cross-framed safety is stiffened by a tubular stay from the neck to the saddle-post, as well as the usual fore-and-aft stays below.

81. Presland and Nelson show three safeties cross-framed, with stiff stays above and below, making a very neat light roadster. Also the "Marvel" rational ordinary, which looks an exceedingly practical mount with any degree of go in it. Well constructed and finished machine altogether, and a credit to such young people.

82. Trigwell and Co.—The name of Trigwell is so intimately associated with ordinaries that we instinctively looked first of all at the ball wheels on this stand, which have needed no variation from last year's perfect details. The safeties are on the curved parallel-tube principle, forming a double tubular quadrilateral frame, with few joints, the crank bracket sliding by means of annular split lugs on the bottom pair of tubes, two small nutted rods drawing the bracket back and forth. Trigwell's well-tried ball-centre head is adapted to the safeties, and some light patterns of racers and semi-racers display considerable ingenuity in the way of fitting light stiffening-pieces across the corners of the frame, hollow Γ pins to the saddle, &c. No better or more reliable machines are made than the "Regent," and for actual merit the exhibit, though small, is second to none.

83. Frank H. Parkyn.—This Wolverhampton maker has found a great run on his Nos. 1 and 2 cross-framed safeties at ten and twelve guineas respectively; they are strongly built for heavy work. The "Olympic" diamond-framed safety, No. 3, has its lower back-fork so arranged as to give a wide bearing at the crank axle and to have the driving-wheel bearing outside the chain-wheel, the tubes of the fork being consequently quite parallel instead of V planned, and joining by a semicircle in front of the crank bearings. The tubes of the frame are otherwise kept in straight lines, and good long centres are used for steering. The down strut is formed of two diagonal tubes. The "Granville" tricycle has a cross-frame with long axle bridge and four bearings, the frame being stayed fore and aft, and looks well worth the £17 10s. asked for it. For ladies, the No. 2 Granville, at £18, is a similar tricycle, but with dropped frame. This maker also has done much to raise the reputation of Wolverhampton work.

84. Buckingham and Adams, Limited.—This reconstructed firm exhibits a large stand of wheels at a disadvantage, the task of designing and making thirty-three new patterns within four months having so severely taxed F. S. Buckingham's resources that at the last moment the show samples could only be indifferently finished. The "Knockmaroon" safety was the first to attract our attention; it is diamond-framed, and made with either socket or very long centre steering, at eighteen guineas. The "Buckingham" safeties are in four varieties of weight, from racer to strong roadster, all with double-tube diamond frames. Semi-diamond and cross framed safeties are also on view, and all have the slotted back-fork ends furnished with Buckingham's patent chain adjustment, which consists of a simple flat eccentric so small as to be not noticed until pointed out, arranged so as to control the movement of the back-wheel spindle in the fork slot. Another peculiarity of the centre-steering machines is that the bottom of the steering post is belled out where it joins the fork-top, instead of terminating in corners,—which imparts strength to this vital point of a safety's steering-gear. Only one pattern of roadster, and one racer, tricycle, is made, this being level wheeled thirty-inch, drop-framed and with detachable stay, Mr. Buckingham telling us that he found very little demand for any other pattern of three-wheeler.

85. J. and H. Brookes.—A large exhibit, principally consisting of good, strong, serviceable safeties, at very moderate prices, considering the undoubted merits of the machines. The No. 1 is a cross-framed safety with a swing bracket for chain adjustment. It is regulated simply by turning a milled nut with the fingers. The patent concealed brake, which is an extremely neat and effective affair, is also fitted, and the machine is a nice businesslike one, and cheap at the price, £17. The No. 2 is very similar, except that the chain tension is adjusted by slots in the fork ends. The No. 5 is also of the cross-framed pattern, but has a strong stay from seat pillar to steering post, and is fitted with tangent spokes. It is a very high-class looking machine. The No. 6 has also a cross frame, but with socket steering, and has a strong tubular stay from seat pillar to steering post. The frame is extra strong, and has a patent swing bottom bracket. This machine, we would say, is specially suited for rough work; and, in fact, it has been designed for Irish roads. The No. 8 is a diamond frame with double tubular cross stay and a very rigid bracket. It has centre steering and the patent concealed brake. The No. 10 has a semi-diamond frame with strong tubular upper stay. The steering is centre. A novel chain adjustment which has been patented by the firm is fitted. The back wheel is carried by the lower end of perpendicular radial fork. This radial fork works on a centre in the end of the horizontal back fork; when, therefore, the upper end of the radial fork is moved along the curved tube, which is concentricle with the back wheel, the lower end travels in the contrary direction, thus adjusting the chain most accurately. The Brookes' direct steering tricycle is a neat drop frame, the strength of which is vastly increased by a stay running from the bottom of the seat pillar forward to the main frame, but not so high as to render the machine unsuitable for a lady. The great novelty about it is the new chain adjustment. It is accomplished by moving the axle round the bridge. The lug which holds the bridge is slackened, when the bridge can be revolved, thus tightening the chain. The lug is then tightened up, and the bridge secured in position. The hind wheel is secured to the bridge by turning it. This operation can be

performed in the simplest possible manner. Another pattern of tricycle is made with front wheel steering *à la* the old "Dublin," and with diamond frame, the upper stay of which can be detached when the machine is required for a lady's use.

86. **Raleigh Cycle Co.**—This is an exceptionally nice exhibit. The machines are all light in comparison to their strength. The designs are excellent, and the finish and turn-out good. The price also is exceedingly moderate. We specially noted the new chain adjustment, by means of which the chain tension can be regulated by simply loosening the hind wheel nuts and turning a screw with the fingers. Their driving wheel is also a speciality, eight spokes being made tangent and the others direct. We also note that they fix the step above the axle, thus getting over the danger of the foot catching on the axle nut. A great number of safeties are shown. The Raleigh "M" is a light roadster with 25-inch wheels, and splendid diamond frame and socket steering, and weighing under 40lbs. The Raleigh "E" has 30-inch wheels. The Raleigh "R" is fitted with the firm's anti-vibration fork and hind wheel spoon brake, and is a staunch roadster, weighing something over 40lbs. The "D" and "S" are still stronger patterns, such as would be most suitable for our roads. The Raleigh "H" is the firm's Irish pattern. It has the diamond frame without anti-vibrator and is a very perfect machine; weight about 45lbs., and price £17 17s. A lady's safety is made which is exceedingly neat, and the main frame of which consists of two tubes running parallel to each other until near the steering post, when the upper tube runs upward, meeting the steering post about a foot from the lower. This gives one of the strongest frames for a lady's safety we have seen in the show. The tandem safety has a similar frame forward, and behind it is exceedingly strongly stayed. This machine also struck us very favourably. In tricycles, two patterns are shown, both with drop frames with a stay running from top of steering post to the angle. One has front wheel spoon brake and the other a band. All the spoon brakes fitted to the "Raleigh" machines are immensely powerful, and their safeties are fitted with patent changeable gear, enabling a purchaser at an extra cost of 7s. 6d. to have an extra gear wheel which he can change in a few moments, according to the nature of the roads or the weather. The firm are also fitting pneumatic tyres, and exhibit a safety so fitted, built to the order of R. J. Mecredy.

86a. **G. and H. Panzetta** have a stall of lamps, spanners, and other sundries, including a spring lamp-bracket of uncommon construction.

86b. **Holophote Cycle Lamp Co.**—Under this peculiar name, a lamp of highly original construction is introduced, which, whatever its merits may be, has at least the virtue of not being the slavish copy of somebody else's inventions which a great many cycle lamps undoubtedly are. The light given by the "Holophote" is somewhat like that of a bullseye, but the glass is a double-convex lens, sloped to point downward or to the road in front, and the comical reflector behind it is un-usually deep. Behind the flame the usual back-reflector is concaved so as to concentrate the rays within the scope of the lens; the reservoir is unusually large, and made so as to be instantaneously detachable from the bottom of the lamp. The socket, too, is constructed so as to allow the lamp to tilt at any desired angle.

87. **W. J. Flather.**—This exhibit consists mainly of specimens of tool steel, and similar material mainly interesting to the trade; but on a counter are shown some spokes, of exceptionally tough quality, which the attendants bend and twist all manner of ways in vain endeavours to break the wire.

88. **Bostel and Loosley.**—These well-known purveyors of small accessories do a great trade in brake-holders and mud-clips; and among their recently-acquired lines will be found a preparation called "Anti-Stiff," which is said to strengthen the muscles and remove pain after over-exertion. They have also a variety of such goods as hose-suspenders, scarf-clips, and braces, which must be seen to be appreciated.

88a.—**Burlingham, Jones and Co.**—Here the sole article exhibited consists of Bourne's tyre-cement, for which the attendant shows an astonishing quantity of written orders.

89. **Griffith's Bros.**—The cycle enamel made by this firm, under the "balloon" brand, enjoys a well-deserved popularity, Singer and Company considering it the best they have used it for touching-up repairs. The Lustre Liquid is a thin transparent varnish for coating nickel-plated and bright metals, drying quickly and saving a world of labour in keeping the bright parts free from rust or tarnish.

90. **Walker, James and Co.**—In the search for a perfect lubricating medium, the "Graphite" lubricating oil has been devised as combining the good properties of graphite with oil, the former substance being plainly visible in the form of a fine powder blended with the oil. Gumming and corrosion are said to be foreign to the character of this combination, and another advantage is that it does not run out of bearings so quickly as plain oil would do.

91. **Powell and Hanmer.**—Cycle lamps in various patterns and sizes are found here, from the high-priced "Triumph" and the "Diamond Light" lamps (the latter of which has a glass moulded into concentric diamond projections) down to a head-lamp and a hub-lamp complete with external winders at the ridiculously low price of half-a-crown each.

92. **H. Sheppard and Co.**—This is a firm who do not believe that there are six cyclists in Ireland; but we venture to prognosticate that their opinions will be considerably altered as soon as the merits of their waterproof capes have become known in our somewhat humid climate. "Indispensable" is not a misnomer for these capes, the weight of which is so infinitesimal that the most inveterate luggage-hater can find no excuse for riding abroad without such an one. The cape is made in

a shape we may call conical, a hole at the apex enabling it to be put on over the head, fastening at the neck with a single hook and eye. Thus there is no gaping join to let the rain in. It is guaranteed waterproof, although so thin, and is ventilated at the back. Being long in front, it can be held down over the handlebar, affording considerable shelter to the knees ; and its open character makes it preferable hygienically to a close jacket. The same material is used for hand-made saddle-covers on the "bathing cap" plan to protect saddles from rain.

93. **Signal Cyclometer Co.**— One of the few cyclometers which have survived the experiences of the year is the "Signal ;" and in addition to the original and the improved patterns, a special style is made for safety-wheels, narrower than usual, and recording only up to 100 miles at a time. The figures "jump" at the end of each mile, simultaneously with the stroke of the signal gong, so that no error in reading is likely to occur.

94. **J. B. Brookes and Co.**—Higher praise could scarcely be given to the goods displayed on this stall than is embodied in the simple tale that we spent an aggregate of over half an hour in three separate visits, vainly trying to ascertain "which was which," from the attendant,—so busy was he in selling goods to eager buyers. The B. 70 (for ordinaries) and B. 80 saddles (for safeties and tricycles), we found, were in greatest request ; and a pattern which most took our fancy was the B. 95, which is of the three-coil spring variety, with an extra narrow peak, and an elliptical (instead of circular) coil-spring to the front, to avoid the sides thereof chafing the rider's thighs. Among a vast quantity of well-made luggage bags and wallets, and luggage carriers, both rigid and spring-supported, we found a couple of ratchet brake-holders of strong construction, calculated to stand a lot of usage in relieving the strain of the brake upon the hand on our long mountain slopes. The simpler of the two costs but 4s., and the other, at 8s. 6d., has a locking arrangement, and looks more substantial.

95. **Geo. Salter and Co.**—To give an idea of the immense quantity of springs turned out by these world-renowned "spring and scale makers" would be a difficult task. "Wholesale to the trade" is their chief line, although their excellent goods are sent retail from the factory too. Our front page contains representations of several leading lines in springs, No. 15 having had a stupendous sale among safety makers, and No. 32 being a favourite tricycle spring. Either of these can be used on the top of a straight seat stalk, or, by aid of the No. 55 socket, on a round ⌐ pin. No. 4 and 62 are springs for ordinary bicycles. No. 31 is a very cheap three-coil spring largely used in the trade ; and No. 60 is a new pattern of combined saddle pin and socket, embodying the fashionable three-coils feature in a way adapted to take any saddle, and with the base wires curved to enable the tilt to be adjusted. The new Registered Trouser Guard is a simple coil of spring steel to be placed around the ankles of a rider who cycles in trousers, the absence of hooks, pin points, or sharp edges, precluding injury to the fabric of the "unmentionables." A

similar spring is made for the coat-collar, to hold the coat in a closed position when unbuttoned. Pedal plates of various patterns are only some of the great many small parts of cycles made by "Salters of Westbromwich."

96. **W. Bown.**—"Bown's bearings bar bicycles being badly built," especially when Bown himself builds the bicycles, as he has now taken to doing for several years past. His latest achievement is one likely to create a great demand, for although the "Aeolus Victor" non-vibrating safety is new to our readers, the spring front-fork which forms the essence of the machine is an American invention, which has stood the test of at least a twelve-month's use across the Atlantic ; and Mr. Bown has improved upon the details so that it is a very practical success indeed. A glance at the illustration on our back page will show the idea in a moment, the woodcut clearly depicting the curved spring-forks with the shackle-joint by which they are connected to the straight rigid forks provided to stiffen the steering. For those riders who do not care about a spring fork, the Aeolus diamond-frame safety is built with all the care which has made the name of Bown a household word wherever cyclists are found ; and such is the demand for these wheels that a considerable addition to the workshops in Summer Lane has been necessitated, the previous accommodation being only sufficient for the manufacture of "bearings and parts" alone.

97. **W. Coote Reynolds.**—Upon coming to this number we found ourselves in the concert-room, where, nevertheless, a number of appreciative spectators were surveying the "Sprite" safeties, among which a "Road Racer" stood prominently forward with nice clean-cut lines and a weight suggestive of pace. The frame is a combination of cross- and semi-diamond, giving a strong truss with little weight. A standard type of trussed-diamond roadster is also on view, the double tubes being connected to the neck in an original manner ; and Laming's patent is used to convert a cross-framed Sprite into an anti-vibrator. The F. pattern of semi diamond roadster looks decidedly cheap at £12, and the H. pattern, trussed-diamond frame with long socket steering, ⅞-inch tyres, and swing bracket chain adjustment, seems quite out of its element at such a low price as £13 10s.

98. **Langton and Co.**—A decidedly handsome machine is the Langton Light Roadster safety ; and in its racing form the same machine looks cut out for pace, the semi-diamond frame taking the saddle well over the driving wheel, a stiff stay connecting saddle post and ball socket head. The Langton Roadster safety, 28 and 30-inch wheeled, and cross-framed, goes as low as £13 10s. ; and the Langton tricycle with ball socket head, four axle-bearings, has its dropped frame stayed above, and is priced at an even twenty pounds.

99. **H. Smith.**—Although we fancy we have heard the name of Smith before, this maker is new to show-goers ; but his exhibits give the idea that

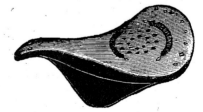

he is well up with the times. The cross-frame is used, with a long top-stay from the steering centres to the saddle, which is in a decided "racing" position far back on top of the rear wheel, the saddle post being curved back to an unusual extent, giving the machine a very rakish appearance. The weight of the racer is stated to be only 18lbs., so that by loosening a nut, and putting the two parts into envelopes, the whole machine could be sent by post, say from John o' Groat's to Castletown-Berehaven, for half-a-crown.

100. **W. Ivy, Rogers and Co.**—The catalogue of the Ivy cycles contains quite a literary curiosity in the shape of some "Hints to Purchasers," which bear upon the face of them so much sound "gumption" that they are worth reproducing here :—

"After deciding to purchase, ascertain the names of one or two makers, and send for their Lists. Give each your careful consideration, and having selected the mount to all appearance suitable, write to a Cycling paper and ask their opinion of the wheel in question. Spend a shilling wisely by testing a few of the testimonials. Enquire of the makers if the vital parts are Steel or Malleable Iron ; if the bearings are hardened and lapped ; and whether tubes or rim steel are used in its construction. Whether you may pay a visit to the works and examine the process of construction, if you happen to be in the district. If the Cycles are warranted for a certain time. Consider the extra advantages offered in a high price machine over the so-called cheap machines. Remember that an extra pound or two wisely spent at the start may bring you much contentment and an article that may be worth £10 more, besides realising its full value if you wish to sell at any time. See that the machine is mechanically, not superfluously, stayed. Remember that the finish of a Cycle, though much to be desired, is a secondary consideration ; also that many a wretched article (not worth its finish) may be, and has been, beautifully finished. If possible, get the best terms by paying cash down. We beg to be allowed to say that the "Ivy," besides being as low in price as is consistent with quality, possesses all the advantages in above hints."

Some originality might reasonably be looked for from the compiler of such an original prospectus ; and we notice many little features in the Ivy justifying the expectation. One point which has not been overlooked is the strengthening of the corners of such frames as the cross-framed Ivy safety by a piece of steel curving across the angle. The Ivy No. 1 has a diamond-frame with curved front tubes; and the entire stock displays points of no little merit.

101. **A. Breese.**—The "Red Cross Harrow" which this agent deals in are very nicely turned out with a semi-diamond frame of original design. From the point where the fore-arm joins the saddle-post, the usual down-tube is replaced by a wide hollow fork carrying the crank bearings outside the chain. Good soft rubbers are fitted by Hookham's process, and the chain is the hardened long-link Abingdon, than which a freer-running chain is not made. The crank-bearings and saddle-post are stayed to the neck ; and the chain adjustment has the Referee screw-check arrangement. A light roadster ordinary is built with Reynolds's triangulated spokes and Hookham's tyres ; and the International saddle is placed further back than usual by aid of a collar, clipped around the backbone to which the front wires are attached, thus enabling the rider to adjust his saddle in any position on the backbone.

102.—**J. Broxup.**—The ordinary bicycle exhibited here is furnished with the interchangeable handles recently described in THE IRISH CYCLIST. For mounting, the usual handlebar is used ; but when once in the saddle the rider can press each half of the bar down into a vertical position, which action causes a secondary pair of handles to arise behind his thighs, thus leaving an open front, to mitigate the dangerous effects of a header.

103. **S. Huxley and Co.** display a tricycle with drop frame made in straight lines, and an almost vertical steering post, carrying a 26-inch steering-wheel in a curved fork. The safeties consist mainly of cross-framed patterns, with curved back and front forks, swing-bracket chain-adjustment, centre steering and continuous steering-posts, the split lug on the centre of the handlebar travelling outside the post. There is a neat semi-diamond frame of peculiar design, the semi-diamond, or triangle, being in front—from neck to down-tube,—and the rear fork being curved as in the cross-framed varieties ; and a diamond-frame with light diagonal struts has a chain-adjustment consisting of a nutted bolt on the cup-and-tube bracket, sliding in a slotted projection from the front of the rear fork. These machines are finished with lines of different coloured gold.

104. **F. W. Wooler.**—Vacant.

105. **Tower Cycle Co.**—Here the "Britannia" lady's safety holds pride of place, and looks remarkably good value at twelve guineas. The front tube curves down in the usual way to the crank bracket, whence the back-fork curves to the rear spindle in the reverse way to that of the stand last previously noticed, the curve of this back-fork dipping in the middle. Stiff tubes go to complete the triangular rear part of the frame, and a strong detachable stay is fitted to enable a male rider to knock the machine about with impunity. The finish altogether is above what might be expected in such a low-priced wheel, and a similar remark might be made with regard to the masculine patterns of this make, which seem indeed to justify the claim that they embody a "Tower of strength." The "Beacon" safety we rather prefer to the Tower Diamond, the latter being on the recognised lines, while the Beacon has a triangular rear-frame, with large diameter down tube and forearm stayed by two compression stays bolted on at either end. A "Robin Hood" safety would make an agreeable and reliable present for a lad, the price being £8 10s., and the finish unexceptionable.

106. **Thomas Beard.**—The first machine to attract attention here is a "Reynard" rational tricycle, with a good big trailing wheel in a curved fork, and a saddle mounted on levers hinged at each end, so as to take play from a pair of tension springs running underneath it, parallel to the backbone. The safeties are all of modern design, comprising strutted diamond frames with centre steering and either swing or slotted crank-brackets, a socket-steering ditto with springs under and over the socket and a curved top tube, and a cross-framed safety at the low price of £17 15s., having such stiff stays from the neck to the saddle pillar and crank bracket as to be almost a semi-diamond. They are well got-up in every way, with good smooth-edged cranks and square rubber pedals on all.

107. **Invicta Machinists' Co.**—Exceptionally staunch in the build is the Invicta tricycle, H pattern, the 30-inch level wheels of which have full inch rubbers and large-guage spokes, drop frame with detachable cross-stay for ladies and the saddle-pillar kept stiff by a curved tube across the angle. Four

axle bearings support the long bridge ; and the price is only £17. A reminder of the good old days is afforded by the Invicta Rational bicycle, on the front forks of which are a pair of the tiny hinged toe-rests with indiarubber rings familiar to our youth. The safeties include the regulation types, the cross-framed having curved back forks.

108. **R. S. Wood** exhibits a sample " W & M " two-speed gear which appears to be a very compact and neat, light two-speed gear. Like all other things of this kind however, it requires the experience of years to determine whether it is sufficiently desirable to be commercially successful.

109. **J. Pollett.**—This also is a two speed gear exhibit of very original construction, and it appears to be a strongly made design and extremely small in construction. It has also the advantage that it can be fitted to any existing crank wheel, and the only doubt in our mind on the subject of its durability is as to whether the shifting arrangement will be found sufficiently strong to withstand the hard work on the road. The price is £3 5s., including fitting to any existing safety or tricycle.

110. **Zimmer and Co.**—Vacant.

111. **W. G. Matthews** shows three safeties devoid of any peculiarity in construction, but well worth the money asked for them.

112. **Samuels and Co.**—These foreign exhibitors' chief line is the Buckjumper safety, which is an ordinary type of safety, but fitted with the Singer patent spring forks, both in front and behind. These forks can be described as being like Keating's patent, but with springs below as well as above the spindle of the wheel to which they are attached. In addition to this spring-framed safety, a number of rigid machines are sold, of everyday types. A racing safety, built with very small diameter tubes, is exceedingly light. A very pretty little juvenile ordinary bicycle is shown. A Cripper tandem tricycle exhibited has very formidable-looking handles for the rear rider, shaped not unlike a very wide capital **U**, so that there is no central post.

113. **Pullinger & Co.**—This go-ahead young firm have a great novelty in the shape of a Triplet tandem safety, convertible into a tandem safety for two riders. This consists of a well-designed tandem safety bicycle of the Lightning type, on to the rear of which a third fork carrying a wheel, crank gear, handles, and saddle, is fitted, with joints so arranged as to allow the rear wheel to rise and fall independently of the front bicycle wheels proper, and to let the rear wheel trail, thus not interfering with the steering. The rear chain, like the chains of the front riders, is geared to the central of the three wheels, which, having to do all the driving, is consequently made extra strong, with the spokes very close together in the rim. The machine shown is not a mere experiment, but has been ridden, and found very speedy and steady in its running. The single " Parade " safeties are of exceedingly light build, calculated to prove very speedy on good roads, and on the path; the one we like best is a close copy of the Referee, but with double tubes from the ball socket head, across which a piece of patent leather is laced to form a light mudguard.

114. **G. Foster.**—Four safeties shown here are all of a very light semi-roadster type, with cross-frames and laced spokes, without brakes and mud-guards, and evidently only intended for " scorching."

115. **Turner, Shute and Co.**—The four safeties shown here are in such an unfinished condition that no criticism can be fairly given.

116. **W J. Cocks.**—The double diamond-frame of this maker's safety is a distinctly original feature, the whole being made of two continuous tubes of small diameter, which start from the back fork end, go straight upward—one on each side of the driving-wheel—to support the saddle, then proceed parallel forward to join the steering-centres, bending down and back to the crank-bearings, and so dividing and returning to the back-fork-ends. Several short bridges connect the tubes during their progress, and a couple of vertical tubes are connected across the diamond. There is no brazing whatever to the frame, the ends being welded to the fork-ends, and the lugs forming bridges are shrunk on. It is decidedly the most original frame in the show, and for a strong roadster its weight is only 9½lbs. Another point of great merit and originality is the ball-socket anti-vibratory head, in which the frame already described is connected to a freely turning ball-socket head, which telescopes over the steering-post, a flexible coil spring inside taking up the jolts of the front wheel. A military safety of this build is exhibited with a rifle slung upon it, and supported by Cockle's patent attachable stand, which takes the form of a rod hinged to the frame near the bottom of the steering-head, and supported when the machine is in motion by a spring catch on the back-fork, and instantly dropped to serve as a support for the machine in a stationary position, a leather-protected chain being also provided, with a padlock, by which the front wheel can be secured from moving.

117. **Eastern Cycle Co.**—These exhibits comprise two safeties without any special points, and a rational ordinary costing only £7 10s.

118. **Vulcan Cycle Co.**—Vacant.

119. **Jelley and Co.**—Enjoying a good reputation locally for very fast light roadsters, this firm's specialité is a " self-steering " head, arranged so that the forks are more raked than the head itself, a principle now adopted by Humber & Co. Another peculiar head is the " Auto," in which the head follows the same angle as the forks, but is an inch in advance thereof, an arrangement which is said to greatly improve the steadiness of the running. A grandly stiff frame is that upon these light roadsters, which are beautifully designed in every respect, and finished in the best possible manner. A light roadster ordinary, with ball-socket head, scales 32lbs, complete with brake and Middlemore's saddle, and looks fast enough to beat road records.

120. **A. Churchill** gives a free insurance policy for £1,000 for a twelvemonth, to every purchaser of one of his cycles, which comprise the three fashionable types of the year, at something under the fashionable price of the year ; and a dashing looking little cross-framed racing safety, should enable its owner, a Catford member, to do good time on Paddington's smooth track.

121. **W. Hewett & Co.** shew a couple of ten guinea safeties, one of which is left quite unpainted, so that spectators can examine the work for themselves, a feature which ought to inspire confidence in the good quality of Hewett's goods.

122. **R. Lovelace.**—There is exhibited on this stall a peculiar but rather meritorious little safety. The driving wheel is 30-inch, and the steering wheel but 24-inch, the spokes being built up in an original fashion, each pair of spokes almost meeting at the rim, the frame built very low for a lady, and the mounting is clearly very easy. A spring luggage carrier fitted to the foot runs in india-rubber lined sockets, and an arrangement to lock the steering acts by means of a rod passing down the steering post with a ring at the top, by which the rod can be raised or lowered. The advantages claimed for it are that it is very easy to mount, the step being placed on the bottom of the

drop frame between the two wheels ; and the head is very narrow.

123. J. Sprunt and Son.—Two "Eagle" safeties, cross-framed, boldly labelled at £10 less 25 per cent. for cash.

124. W. Woolidge claims that his spring-framed Arabian is the lightest in the show. It is on the British Star principle, but instead of the spring used on that machine there are two coil-springs in compression, behind the saddle, surrounding the parallel tubes, which go to make up the upper back-fork, so that there is no lateral play.

125. J. B. Whitgreave.—Of the many contrivances devised from time to time in the way of supports to enable a bicyclist to stand still without dismounting, Whitgreave's patent attachment for a safety is one of the very few that have been found at all practicable. It is not—like most of such devices—a mere crutch, but it consists of a small supplementary wheel 6 inches in diameter, carried on an arm attached to the rear frame of a safety so as to be quite clear of the ground and out of the way. When the rider wishes to stop, or to go very slowly, he merely loosens a wire cord on the handlebar, whereupon the arm carrying the small wheel drops so that the wheel runs on the ground and thus practically converts the safety for the nonce into a tricycle.

126. Samuel A. Gibbs, of Great Yarmouth, shows an ordinary bicycle of common construction with an old idea revived in the shape of the backbone being divided behind the saddle and passing under the saddle in the form of a loop, so that there is no thickness of backbone between the saddle and the wheel. This enables a rider to get closer down to his wheel.

127. Alldays and Onions.—Very elegantly finished cycles are these, denoting great care in attention to little details, even to such trivial points as footrest-rubbers, which are of square section. The tricycles are drop-framed with socket steering and swing crank-brackets, adjusted by means of the back-stays, which pass through holes in the middle of the four-bearing axle-bridge, and have nuts in front and behind the bridge for the purpose. The cross-framed safety with top-stay between the saddle pillar and the neck looks full of strength and go ; and the diamond safeties have anti-vibration springs below and above the steering socket. A semi-diamond-framed safety with centre steering is very elegantly designed and well finished.

128. Taylor, Cooper and Bednell, Ltd.—This firm's trump card must unquestionably be its socket-steering safeties, which are so neat and compact-looking as to deceive the onlooker, the sockets being really fitted with balls ; the plain sockets are also remarkably neat, altogether doing away with the clumsiness frequently associated with socket steering. All the regular types of safeties are shewn from the £10 cross-framed safety to the very complete Model A., and in all cases the details are well worked out, from the shackle-break-spoons to the tapered seat-pillars. Altogether a most promising display, which pressure of time alone prevented us dealing with more fully.

129. August Larsen, Liege.—This Belgian maker introduces some very low-priced safeties, two of which have rather uncommon shaped frames. A diamond frame instead of having the verticle strut has two curved struts of rim steel. Another safety has a cross frame with the addition of vertical back fork connected to the cross by a quarter circle tube. A tricycle is labelled £8 10s., and looks remarkably cheap at the price, until we discovered that it is only a

single driver, and, in fact, nothing but an overgrown juvenile tricycle. Some juvenile safeties complete the exhibit.

130. Morris Cycle Co.—The old fly-wheel ideal is here found adapted to the rear-driving safety, the fly-wheel taking the form of a small solid wheel about six inches in diameter, and two inches thick, which is geared into the driving chain. We are afraid, however, that the latest specimen of the fly-wheel notion will be no more successful than its many predecessors have been.

131. Marriott Cycle Co.—This is a new firm, and their standard pattern is a cross-framed safety, without any very special features worth narrating, except that the top and bottom stays are bolted, instead of otherwise fastened to the neck. The tangent spokes are carried through the hub and going straight to the rim without a bend. The swing bracket for chain tension is secured in a jamb-case.

132. P. W. Davis.—This maker exhibits a light spring tricycle of a rather uncommon design. It is a Cripper, but the rear frame rests upon the bearings of the axle, by means of two flat steel tubes in the shape of an S.

133. Tarver and Bowley.—About the queerest kind of safety bicycle ever built, is the Euclidia, the frame of which looks like nothing more or less than two back wheels. The frame is in fact constructed of rim steel bent into the shape of two irregular circles, and firmly stayed together by spokes, which it is claimed makes an extremely rigid as well as a light and strong frame. However this may be, we must at least award the inventor the cake for originality.

134. W. Williams.—This maker's "Poly" safeties are another class of racing safeties with the saddle right over the back wheel, ball socket head and the backbone constructed of two flat tubes running direct from the head to the back wheel spindle.

135. Austen Bros.—Only two machines are shewn here, both alike, cross framed, light safeties ; one a racer, and the other a semi-racer, or light roadster, built for Mr. R. E. Knight, with a very exaggerated curve to the handlebars, and a new idea is to relieve the frame from its harsh rigidity by putting a very small spring at the bottom end of the front stay so as to allow a trifling amount of give to the frame.

136 Reinhold and Co.—A specialité in wheels is this firm's leading feature, the title being the "Mobilis Radius," and the object of the invention being to preclude the liability of the spokes to break in the hub or sustain uneven strains. This is effected by two separate means, the better being the use of spherical headed nipples, which are passed through holes drilled rather larger than necessary through a flanged hub, the ends of the spokes being screwed into these headed nipples. As the nipples are free to shift slightly in the holes of the hub flange, there is not the commonly-experienced tendency to snapping of the spokes at the point where they screw into the hub. The patent seems good, and the "Mobilis Radius" wheels should be heard of.

137. Armstrong Cycling and Engineering Co., Ltd.—This is another new firm to the cycle trade, and their display, although nothing out of the regular lines, created a decidedly good impression, a Girton ladies' safety being one of the best things on their stand, and some ordinary bicycles, with Abingdon ball heads, being nicely finished and very light roadsters.

138. The Pneumatic Tyre and Booth's Cycle Agency, Limited.—We deal with this exhibit at length as the tyre is undoubtedly a most

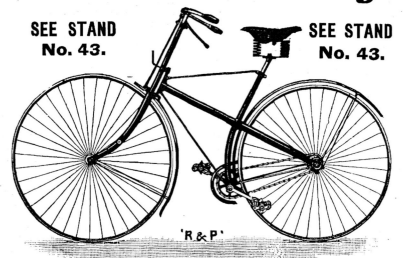

novel and interesting invention, and we have been questioned by so many as to our personal experience that we know it will satisfy our readers. A Pressman recently was kind enough to inform us that the writer (R. J. Mecredy) could not be impartial on the question of the Pneumatic Tyre, because he was connected with the company. Those who are of this opinion need not read this notice ; but we know that the majority of our readers have perfect confidence in our integrity and fairness, and for the benefit of these we will give our own impressions of the tyre, founded on an experience of nearly four months, and backed up by the opinion of Mr. A. J. Wilson, which exactly coincides. with ours. We will face the disadvantages, or alleged disadvantages first. Will the tyre wear ? We are of opinion that it will. No tyre has ever gone wrong during our experiments, neither have we ever noticed the smallest nick, nor jagged edge from riding over metal. One of the machines exhibited has run over a thousand miles on the roughest roads in Ireland, and their is no sign of wear. Will the inner tube cut ? Possibly. A nail or stout thorn may cut it under certain circumstances, but we never saw this accident occur, although we know that it has happened. To effect a repair is very simple. The cost will only be from 1s. to 2s., and any man of ordinary intelligence can be shown how to do it for himself. Replacing broken spokes is another disadvantage which has been much exaggerated, for the tyre can easily be removed in any particular spot. The disadvantage of side-slipping is a more real one. There is a certain amount of suction in the tyre which gives it a better grip on the ground than a solid tyre ; and consequently on greasy setts, or on *thin* mud, or on freshly wetted roads, it is much freer from side-slipping than the solid tyre. On thick mud, however, though the tyre still grips the *surface* firmly, its width prevents it from penetrating, and the *mud* slips on the mud beneath. From this cause the safety is not a good winter machine for country roads, but for eight months of the year *thick* mud is practically non-existent, and we do not think side-slipping will occur often. This is a question we purpose to go into very fully in THE IRISH CYCLIST AND ATHLETE later, even four months' experience during the winter is not sufficient to enable us to speak as definitely as we would like to. Of course this side-slipping question does not affect the tricycle. The last disadvantage which we will deal with is a more serious one. It is the cost. About £5 will be the charge for the tyres for a safety, and of course more for a tricycle ; but apart from the advantages of the tyre, which we deal with below, another point must be taken into consideration. The complete interception of vibration between the rims and the ground saves the machine from all jar and jolt, and consequently it will last much longer and require less repairs than a solid-tyred machine ; and if we mistake not, this will, at least, save the amount of the extra charge. And now, as to the advantages. After careful experiments carried out by the aid of other riders and on all kinds of surfaces, we feel convinced that a "Pneumatic" machine is from half a mile to three miles an hour faster than any other, the difference being greatest on rough roads. Up hill no machine can hold it, and in coasting it runs right away. We make this statement deliberately in the full confidence that it will be borne out during the season. The rider's complete comfort is assured ; the tyres cannot come off, and there is no noise. It follows from its speed that the ease of propulsion is very great, the cause being that obstructions sink into the tyre without checking the momentum, and the machine and rider seem to flow over them. The weight of frames can be much reduced without sacrificing

strength, and the absence of nervous exhaustion caused by vibration will, apart from the ease of propulsion, enable greater journeys to be performed with less fatigue than heretofore. The life and general "go" about a Pneumatic machine is most remarkable. The success of the invention can only have one effect on the trade, and that a good one. Where rough roads prevail, as in Ireland, it will simply double the number of cyclists ; for hundreds give up the sport yearly because of the excessive vibration which affects the spine and causes nervous headache, or because the labour and actual discomfort over rough roads is so very great. All first-class makers will reap the advantage, for the invention is no monopoly. On the other hand, it never can become general, for the high price puts it beyond the reach of the majority, and it cannot affect, in any way, the sale of cheap machines, and even on spring frame machines it will form a valuable addition, the latter counteracting the effect of wavy surfaces and big holes, which give a heavy jolt, though no sharp jar, to a rigid Pneumatic machine. The Company exhibit a Singer Tricycle and "New Rapid," "Irwell," "Humber," and "Whippet Safeties," and besides these makers, Messrs. Morris, Wilson and Co., The Raleigh Cycle Co., The Pilot Cycle Co., The Success Cycle Co., Messrs. Bayliss, Thomas and Co., Messrs. Townsend, and Messrs. Ellis and Co., are open to receive orders to our personal knowledge ; doubtless there are others also.

139. **W. Patmore.**—A nice exhibit of very cheap machines. The No. 1 is a semi-diamond frame safety with tubular stay from seat pillar to neck, and slot adjustment. It is a neat, strong machine, nicely turned out, and selling at £16 10s. The No. 2 has the diamond frame with cross stay, and a second cross stay within a few inches of the steering post. The steering is socket, and the tread is exceedingly rigid. A good plunger brake is fitted, and the weight, all on, is only about 40lbs. The "Rocket" spring frame has a semi-diamond frame, and is fitted with Laming's patent joint. A special pattern meant for the Irish roads has ⅞in. tyres, and is strongly built throughout, and sells at the wonderfully low price of £10, while a good, strong-looking cross-framed safety is listed at £7 10s. The greatest novelty in this exhibit is the "Simplex" convertible Tandem, which in many respects is similar to that exhibited on the Humber stand. The front portion is an ordinary direct steering tricycle, to which is hinged a steering post with cups to receive the centres of a rear steering safety. By means of the attachment any safety and tricycle can thus be converted into an excellent tandem, and this combination has an advantage over that exhibited by Messrs. Humber, in that it is not necessary to have a special rear portion for attachment. There is a decided future before this machine, and the price of the whole complete is £26, or including the front wheel to complete the safety, £30. At this price there should be a ready demand, for it is really very moderate, comprising as it does a complete tricycle, a complete safety, and a complete tandem.

140. **Civil and Military Cycle Supply.**—A very nice semi-diamond frame is here exhibited, with crank-axle bracket sliding on extensions of the rear stays, this arrangement giving a firm and rigid tread ; tangent spokes are fitted. The steering is central. The driving wheel is 28in. and the front wheel 30in., and the weight complete under 40lbs. It is really a taking machine and nicely finished. A cross-framed pattern is also shown, strongly stayed above and below, and fitted with 30in. wheels. Military cycles are the speciality of the firm. A strong cross-framed safety is shown, with arrangement for carrying rifle, &c., and a contrivance enabling it to remain stationary should

PARADE CYCLES

Are made specially for Irish Roads, with 7-8 and 3-4 Wheels, and weigh only 40lbs.

PARADE No. 1.   **PARADE No. 2.**

Inspect the Machines at the Stanley Show before placing your orders. Best material only used. No extras. Write for Price Lists to

PULLINGER & CO.,

PARADE CYCLE WORKS, HEREFORD PLACE, NEW CROSS, LONDON.

Important to Agents and Dealers.

Don't fail to see "Cycledom's" Exhibits,

Stanley Show, STAND 25, (near the Stage)

For Latest Pattern Cycles.

STAND 162, (near the Stage)

For all classes Cycle Fittings, Rough and Finished.

Trade Supplied.

CYCLEDOM,

53, 54, & 55, Blackfriars' Road, LONDON, E.C.

Steam Works—COLLINGWOOD STREET, BLACKFRIARS.

600

SAFETY AND OTHER CYCLES.

Special Job Lines to Agents.

Absolute Clearance Sale during Stanley Show.

NICKEL PLATING & ENAMELLING.

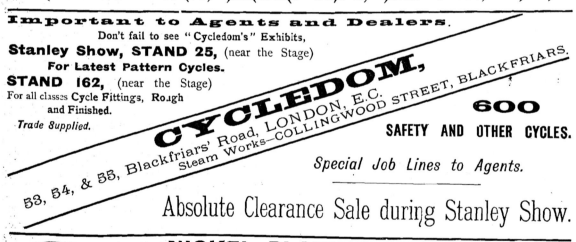

SILLS & Co.

The Largest and Oldest Platers and Enamellers to the Cycle Trade in England.

PROMPT ATTENTION PAID TO ALL AGENTS' ORDERS.

Gold, Silver & Nickel Platers,
Enamellers, Liners, etc., } **COVENTRY.**

the rider so desire. Two of these safeties are exhibited connected together to form a sociable somewhat in the same manner as the " Twin," but the connections are rather simpler, and can be easily taken apart. The exhibit is on the whole a good one.

141. Harry S. Roberts.—The Special safety No. 1 has the diamond frame with cross stay, and a particularly rigid bracket. The lower chain wheel is between the bearing boxes, and Perry's hubs, spokes, and cranks, are fitted. The steering is ball socket, and the finish and general turnout is very neat and business like. The price is £16 10s. The No. 2 has centre steering. It is a strong, neat machine of almost similar design, selling at £14. The No. 3 is similar to the last machine, with the exception of the absence of the cross stay, and sells at £12 10s. Another pattern of the safety is made with a semi-diamond frame, with a splendidly rigid bracket. The cross-frame is also used with a tubular stay from seat pillar to steering centre, and two cheap patterns of this machine are turned out at £11 10s. and £8 10s. respectively, both excellent value for the money. A very neat Juvenile safety sells at £6 10s. The Special bicycle No. 2, with drop frame and 30in. wheels, is listed at £16 10s. The exhibit is altogeather an excellent one and very creditable to the maker.

142. Start Cycle Co.—The "Start" diamond-framed safety is a very strong machine with cross stay and socket steering, the upper and lower tubes being carried well apart. The bracket is rigid, and double tubes run from crank axle bearing boxes to the steering post; price £16. A light roadster of the same pattern is made with hollow rims and tangent spokes. A diamond frame is also made with centre steering, and without a cross stay, and selling at the marvellously low price of £7 10s., by no means a badly finished machine, and at the price simply wonderful. The new "Start" safety is a cross frame, well stayed above and below, and selling at £12 10s. Patterns on somewhat similar lines sell at £10 and £7 10s. respectively.

143. L. S. Haskins.—Another marvellously cheap lot of machines. The "Perfect" No. 1 has a diamond frame with centre steering, and is nicely finished. The No. 2 has also a diamond frame with centre steering, and sells at £18 18s. The No. 3 has a semi-diamond frame, with tubular stay from steering post to neck. The tread is rigid, and the machine altogether a strong one. Price £9 18s. The No. 4 is a cross frame, and sells at £7 10s. A very neat ladies' safety is listed at 10 guineas. These machines are all finished in very nice style, and look well.

144. F. Malache and Co.—Another exhibit of cheap machines. A cross frame safety is shown at £5 10s., and a semi-diamond at £9. There is also a good-looking diamond frame, and another diamond frame pattern, with double parallel tubes running direct from neck to hind wheel centre, and from hind wheel centre upwards to neck. It is listed at 13 guineas.

145. J. Wooster.—The "Surrey" wheeler roadster safety is distinguished by an exceedingly neat socket ball head. The frame is a semi-diamond, the steering post curving far back over the driving wheel. The "Victoria" tricycle is a cross-framed machine with top stay from centres to seat pillar; and the back stays between the crank-shaft and the axle-bridge instead of running parallel are crossed. A ladies' tricycle is also shown with an effective dress guard, butt-ended spokes, and Perry's axle; and a "Victoria"

racing tricycle is built with Perry's light axle and bearings.

146. Doughty.—Only two machines were staged here; the "Granville" light roadster safety being a cross-framed machine with duplex flat tubes for the backbone. A diamond frame "Granville" safety is decidedly cheap at £8 10s.

147. Fred Cooke.—The solitary safety shown by the sole agent for the Ulma bells is a Juvenile safety with a frame built of continuous steel rod, so that [upon] concussion the force of the blow is distributed. The rods are kept apart by stampings, and the principle of construction enables these machines to be sold at the phenomenally low price of £3 10s. A tricycle on similar lines was to have been shown, but was not ready.

148. Frederick Baxter.—The "Samson" is the name of this maker's cross-framed safety, which is capitally stayed in every direction, selling at £8 15s. A tricycle of the same name exactly resembles the first "Ivel" cross-framed tricycle, the fork forming the back part of the cross-frame being attached to the axle by means 9t slots bolted to the axle bridge, the slots giving adjustment for wear of the chain. ||

149. J. Howes and Sons.—There was no one in attendance at this stand when we examined the machines shown, and we could therefore not make enquiries, but to all appearances the safety "Gorantie" was built for a giant of some 8 feet in height, the 33in. wheels supporting a diamond frame of such heroic dimensions as to be quite impracticable for a man of ordinary size.

150. Smith and Molesworth.—A discount of 40 per cent. on a single machine, or of 50 per cent. on large orders, is the attraction offered by these people to purchasers of their "Alert" safeties, and considering the exceptionally low prices at which they are listed it is difficult to understand how they can do it ! The patterns present, cross-framed, diamond-framed, and semi-diamond safeties, as well as drop-framed tricycles, offer a great variety of choice to those seeking after something exceptionally cheap.

151. William Mansell.—This is one of the rather numerous makers who fancy the name "Dart" for a trade mark, and he shows well-stayed cross-framed safeties, both finished and in the bare metal, as well as a convertible Dart safety, which, by the removal of the top bar, can be converted into a first rate ladies' safety

152. Fly Cycle Co.—"Thoroughly up to the times" is a phrase synonymous with the slang term of "fly ;" and in the case of the "Fly" cycles we find safeties made up to the latest developments, including ball socket head, and listed at £17 10s. The "Great Eastern" ladies' safety, with a semi-diamond frame and ball steering, has an unusually long wheel-base, giving ample accommodation for a lady's dress between the wheels.

153. Iroquois Cycle Co.—These makers are nothing if not original, and their latest varieties of "Minnehaha" safeties are built of small section tubes put together on novel lines ; thus the handle-bars and front fork consist of two continuous tubes, and the whole frame is built up of small diameter tubing in such a way as to secure an exceedingly light frame. It is guaranteed to carry a 16 stone rider, although weighing only 28 lbs. A ladies' safety is made on a similar principle with triangular back frame, and instead of a single pair of tubes connecting the steering post and the crank bracket, there are first one pair of straight tubes from the crank bracket to the steering post, and then a second tube centrally springs up from a few inches in front of the crank bracket, and joins the top of the steering post, thus strengthening the

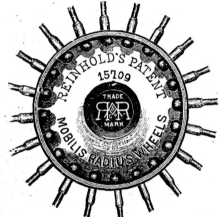

crank bracket in a way that would not be possible without such secondary tube. The roadster safety beforementioned is also found converted into a tandem bicycle, a saddle being mounted exactly over the front wheel spindle, provided with handles, and a crank bracket being supported by secondary forks in front of the front wheel, an arrangement which we are afraid will be found not to give at all steady steering, but which the manager of the firm thinks will be practicable, the small size of the front wheel removing some of the objections based upon our own experience of a similar type of tandem with a 36-inch front wheel.

154. **St. George's Cycle Co.**—This firm must not be mistaken for the old-established St. George's Engineering Co. "Impetus" is the name of the safeties exhibited, which are on regular lines, an endeavour being made to keep the parallel tubes of frames as wide apart as possible, for the sake of lateral strength.

155. **Weald and Crescent Cycle Co.**—Here the great feature is another demonstration of the continuous tube frame safety, but in this case the shape is not curved, but bent angles following a diamond shape, with two pairs of vertical struts stiffening it. The steering post is some inches behind the front fork top, ball socket steering being fitted. It is a very light and effective hill-climber.

156. **F. Haisman and Co.**—Although handicapped by a bad position, in a dark corner, the Byrne-Haisman cycles deservedly attract a great deal of attention, having points of radical novelty such as are always associated with the name of their inventors. No less than £1,300, we are informed, has been expended in bringing the Byrne-Haisman balance-framed safety and tricycle to their present degree of perfection. The principle is totally unlike any other machine, more resembling the Spinaway swing frame than anything else we can think of. The safety has a cross frame, but not rigidly crossed, the backbone being formed of duplex flat tubes, between which the tubular saddle pillar is mounted by a hinge-joint at the crank bracket, a spring midway controlling the forward play. Thus the saddle can be swung forward, as was the case with the Spinaway, automatically adjusting the action to suit the gradient. A similar action, but varied in its structural details, is adapted to the tricycle. There is no *downward* give of the frame whatever. Standard types of rigid safeties, with cross and segmental frames, have a double cogged driving hub whereby the gearing can be quickly changed, a very simple and quick-acting adjustment to the back wheel spindle, facilitating removal of the wheel for this purpose. Revolving brushes are mounted on a pliable spring designed for attachment to the back fork of a safety, in such a way that the brushes rest against each side of the driving chain, cleansing it of dirt without applying any retarding friction; and a special dry lubricant is sold for use with the brushes.

157. **S. Rowe and Co.**—The prevailing type of "Paragon" safety is a kind of cross-frame, but the front part of the cross is quite horizontal, the rear fork being consequently more upright than is usual. The steering-post, too, is nearly vertical, the front fork having consequently to be much curved forward to the front wheel spindle, with the result claimed that it does not skid.

158. **John Warrick.**—Carrier tricycles form the staple article on this stand, the Monarch system of driving adapting itself readily to the necessities of weight-carrying. There is no chain or other gearing-up appliance, but the cranked axle has stirrup pedals dependant from it, the gear thus being low with freedom from a lot of the friction inseparable from ordinary systems of driving. Boxes to suit various trades

are mounted behind the rider, and the steering-wheel is in the extreme rear, its fork having a cradle-spring-like arrangement to intercept jolting. One uncommon arrangement consists of a carrier for a fishmonger, ventilated at the sides, and provided with an ice-tray low down close to the ground.

159. **Abingdon Works Co.**—The handsome show-cases of this first-class firm contain samples of the beautifully finished parts of cycles which are so largely used in the trade, the name of the Abingdon chains being proverbial. Whilst the "Abingdon Humber" pattern of chain is preferred by an immense number of makers and riders, we have always personally had a preference for the hardened open-link chain, which we have found to run with a remarkable absence of that grinding friction peculiar to other patterns of chains as soon as the teeth of driving pulleys commence to wear. With the open-link chain, a certain amount of stiffness for the first hundred miles or so has hitherto been a drawback, but this objection is now removed, the chain being made up less tightly than of yore, so that it runs freely from the very first. The Abingdon patent ball-head, differential gear, detachable cranks, King Dick wrench, and other small fittings, are too well known to need description. Agents and small makers wanting ready-made parts of unexceptionable quality, cannot do better than buy from the Abingdon Works Company.

160. **W. Middlemore.**—Since the firm of John Harrington & Co. was merged in that of W. Middlemore, the combination of the principle of the Cradle spring with that of Middlemore's saddles has been thoroughly effected, although even the good old "Cradle" is still in demand. The development of the coil-wire principle, in conjunction with the fore-and-aft swinging action of shackles, is seen to advantage in the "Cradle Saddle," which has, in its turn, been now altered by the substitution of two conical coil springs for the rear shackle. A very favourite spring-saddle among road scorchers is the "Cone-Combination" saddle, the leather of which is supported on three conical coil springs, which bear on a light frame, the whole being of a very slight weight. A number of the very best makers are fitting this and it may be seen in most of the stands. Beside saddles, we noticed some very nice square cases for cameras, and long ditto for carrying folding tripods, the leather being stiff so as to retain its shape, and facilitate rapid removal and replacement of the contents.

161. **F. Brampton and Co.** display samples of their well-known driving chains, in a show case.

161. **Cycledom's** stall of sundries is well supplied with every kind of small goods such as bells, spanners, horns, a whistle with rubber ball to blow it, &c. Here also are found Southard's patent cranks, which have made such a stir in the trade lately, the strength being demonstrated daily by means of heavy weights being hung on the end of a crank firmly secured to a bench. If for their neat appearance alone, Southard's cranks deserve attention, but we believe their unbreakable qualities to be well proven by actual use on the road.

163. **Clough and Carter.**—A good deal has been heard lately of a two-speed gearing brought out by these Bradford engineers; but although a safety was exhibited with the apparatus fitted, it was so hidden away in an inaccessible nook that we could gleam no idea of its construction.

164 **Cycle Record.**—Our youngest contemporary advertises itself well by distributing large quantities of Lilliputian pamphlets containing lists of road and path records.

165. **Henry Lees.**—Since we first met this maker at the Agricultural Hall, strolling about with

STANLEY SHOW, 1890.

Those seeking one of the greatest Novelties in the show, with strength and
utility combined, will find it in the

SOUTHARD CRANK,

To be seen tested each day at **Cycledom's Stand, 162,** at 3 p.m. Also
attached to Machines at the following Makers' stands, who will be pleased to supply
same:—Humber and Co.; Cycledom, 25; Linley and Biggs; Morris and Wilson;
Success Cycle Co.; Taragni, Holt and Co.; Midland Cycle Co.; Ford and Co.;
St. George's Cycle Co.; etc., etc. Pronounced to be the strongest, lightest, neatest,
cheapest, most reliable and convenient Crank. Made to suit all Machines. Keying
on or *detachable King Dick Patent*, with long or short slot for pedal adjustment.

N.B.—These Cranks are rapidly replacing the
old style of Crank. See your maker undertakes
to supply same when ordering your new machine.

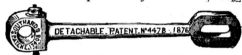

The "SPECIAL"

his new stop bell, the "Facile" has occupied a prominent place in its class, and quite ousted the old sleigh-bell or "jingler" from popular favour. It is certainly the neatest, and most durable, bell on the market.

166. **W. Carson and Sons** occupy a small stand with two samples of Keating's spring luggage-carrier which is so much used by amateur photographers. One of these, we see, is hinged at the angle of the frame so that when not in use it can be folded up ; and also, we fancy, so that tight strapping will not tend to squeeze the **L** frame permanently out of a right angle. We can recommend the carrier most strongly from personal experience. For a camera, certainly nothing can beat it.

167. **Fly Cycle Co.**—A stall furnished with gun metal and steel hubs, toe-clips, adjustable foot rests, and other small parts.

168. **George Norris.**—Since the "Anglo-Dutchman" first called the attention of cyclists to the virtues of Norris's horse-skin shoes, we have been wearing them continually for both riding and walking; and when we say that they are faultless we have passed a high encomium upon them. Varying as they do in price, the highest quality of cycling shoe is made with a strip of steel along the sole which prevents any irregular wear being caused by rat-trap pedals or peculiarity of tread, and the enhanced durability—to say nothing of the beauty and comfort—of the shoes fully compensates for the rather high cost.

169. **Sport and Play.**—This Birmingham athletic paper laid itself out regardless, by sending a real live Wheelwright to criticise the show on its behalf.

170. **Samson, Teale and Co.**—Show-cases containing fittings and small parts of cycles, as supplied to the trade.

171. **George Townsend and Co**—The greatest novelty in this stall is the No. 1 Ecossais safety. It has a magnificent double-diamond frame with hinged adjustment bracket and 28in. tangent wheels. The steering is centre, and the machine is a handsome one, and with every appearance of great strength, though it scales under 40lbs., all on. One of this pattern is also exhibited fitted with pneumatic tyres, for which it is eminently suitable. The No. 2 is also diamond frame, with either socket or centre steering. It is a strong, serviceable mount, and one which we tested very severely before Christmas. We found that it wore splendidly, ran easily, and was absolutely free from side-slip. We were riding it for weeks and it gave complete satisfaction. The chain adjustment is by means of a sliding bracket. The Ecossais Telescopic safety is a cross-frame, stayed above and below, and with socket steering. Another pattern is made with 28in. wheels and socket steering, and sells at the very low price of £12. The firm also make a ladies' safety with an adjustable stay and tangent wheels. The Ecossais tricycle is a very neat machine, with drop frame and the same chain adjustment as in the safety. The firm also put a tandem in the market this season, very strongly stayed, with good rigid tread, and with ball pedals, &c., selling at £30. The firm also make great quantities of parts and frames for the trade. This season they have done a very large business in Ireland, and from the great improvement made in this years' patterns, especially in the introduction of lighter patterns, the weight having been very much cut down, we anticipate they will do still better.

172. **Wheeling.**—In addition to copies of itself, our London contemporary disposes of quantities of maps, photos, and copies of *The Young Man*, the latter being repeatedly sold in the most heartless way by the young woman in charge.

173. **The Irish Cyclist and Athlete.**—Next door to *Wheeling*, but divided from it by a huge statue, stands a noble architectural erection which some ribald individual pretended to take for one of Ellis's portable Turkish Baths. This was in reality the stand whereupon were displayed, in all their pristine beauty, copies of our current issue, of *Duffersville*, of *The Jarvey*, of *Two Trips to the Emerald Isle*, and of various other high-toned publications of which for further particulars see small bills That is to say, these priceless literary specimens were displayed thereon as long as a sweet-voiced and blue-eyed youth was about, but such was the demand for them that we grieve to state that the British public appropriated more copies than they paid for, when the aforesaid guardian angel wasn't looking. Contiguous to the Portable Tur—we mean the stall,— was an enclosed office wherein the Editor and the Manager of this periodical essayed to obtain fleeting intervals of freedom from the old-friends-from-the-country who *would* talk, and where a phonographic assistant from the Metropolitan School of Shorthand was immured from foggy morn to windy eve, grinding out reams of strokes and pot-hooks from dictation. As we found—too late for rectification,—that this youth was ignorant of the difference between a hub and a pub, a butt-ended spoke and a buttered scone, a handlebar and a refreshment bar, or between any of the other details of construction which we perseveringly fired at him, we have to trust to luck for his transcription of our hurried notes at all resembling what we meant to convey.

174. **Le Veloce Sport.**—Our French contemporary's stall was cheek-by-jowl with our office, and adorned by the colours of La Republique Francais, and the portraits of a marvellously important-looking staff of editors, correspondents, and representatives of various sorts, causing us to wonder how we in Dublin can possibly contrive to get along with a literary staff of four men and a dog.

175. **Iliffe and Son.**—The London publishers of the Coventry papers had a large stall of *The Cyclist* and *Bicycling News*, as well as the ample variety of books which are published by the Iliffes.

176. **Herbert and Hubbard.**—Among a good assortment of samples of cold drawn weldless steel tube, mudguards, and chain guards, some mudguards expressly made for pneumatic-tyred machines, an indication that this firm is fully alive to the probable demand for such goods.

177. **F. Haslam**, in addition to a great variety of rubber tyres, handles, handle covers, and cement, shows a three bar rubber pedal.

178. **Silico Enamel Co.**—For a great many years, various attempts have been made to produce a transparent varnish suitable for coating the bright parts of cycles ; but so unsatisfactory were the earlier preparations that the task appeared to have been given up as hopeless until the "Silico Enamel" was brought out, since the furore created by this highly successful competion has caused many imitations to spring up. We have had our own cycles coated on all the nickelled parts, with the Silico, for over a year, now, and such is its perfection that we have made it a rule to apply it to every new machine we purchase, before the pristine beauty of the nickel has been dulled. It is not generally understood that nickel-silver is, although a protective of steel to a certain extent, yet so porus in its nature that moisture eats through it and rusts the steel beneath ; hence the rapidity with which nickelled handlebars, cranks, etc. shew signs of rustiness. The "Silico" enamel prevents this by impalpably varnishing the nickel ; and so thin and transparent is it that the brightness of the nickel is not in any way dulled. Being so thin, too

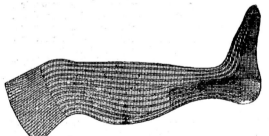

a very little of it goes a long way, so that it is economical in use. In our moist Irish climate, nobody should buy a cycle without immediateley coating it with this excellent rust-preventing solution.

179. **J. L. Hancock.**—This veteran maker of rubber tyres is as prominently to the fore as ever with samples of the "caoutchouc" goods for which his name is famous.

180. **Wilkins and Co.** have a small stand containing the various parts and accessories in which they deal, supplying the London trade largely.

181. **Thos. Smith & Sons, Ltd.**—Stampings and castings constitute the *magnum opus* of " Smiths o' Saltley, who take justifiable pride in announcing that they are the actual producers, and can therefore supply the trade with parts and accessories at rock-bottom prices."

182. **P. Vaughton and Sons.**—Medals and challenge-shields, such as are calculated to make the laziest Ohne Hast rider experience an inward desire to covet the victories of the race-path, are supplied in vast quantities by the Vaughtons, who also furnish the badges which adorn the caps of an immense army of clubmen. Their exhibit consists of samples of these goods, which are most worthy examples of artistic jewellery. Name-plates for cycle-makers are another line in which a great trade is done ; and anyone wanting this class of goods cannot do better than obtain estimates from this celebrated firm of manufacturing jewellers.

183. **A W. Gamage.**—Sanitary wool clothing, gloves, waterproofs, racing costumes, and shoes, are here found in perfection, racing drawers in any colour being sold at the ridiculously low price of eighteenpence a pair. The referee racing shoe is a beautifully light article, constructed of thin horse-skin, with patent holes for the laces, and costing half a guinea the pair. The "Scotia" web-wool breeches are warm and highly hygienic.

184. **John Pollit.**—The "Collier" change-gear ; vide 109.

185. **H. Renold.**—This is a show-case containing examples of Renold's well-known chains, including the new "Non-Stretchable" pattern.

186. **E. Harrison and Co.**—Tailoring and hosiery of various descriptions are seen to here, the elastic-web clothing being a line in which the firm has a very long experience.

187. **Hutchins, Hamilton and Co.**—Since last year, the Home Trainers with large dials, for racing purposes, have been further improved, and their mechanism is so simple and substantial as not to be at all likely to get out of order. A new type is now made for a single rider to obtain pedalling practice on a machine having a degree of resistance closely approximating to that of actual path-racing, which much be far more useful than the mere quick pedalling features hitherto associated with home-trainers ; this is accomplished by mounting a spider wheel in a frame, and gearing it up very highly by means of a chain ; an indicating dial telling the rider how he is going. For club-rooms and cycle-agencies no better attraction can be found, and the makers are exceedingly busy in supplying the continual demand for the apparatus. For ordinary bicycles, too, these veteran cyclists fit a Middlemore's saddle with a capital link, whereby it can be adjusted to any one of three positions on the backbone,—an addition which will be appreciated by lovers of rational ordinaries.

188. **H. Matthews.**—Luggage-carriers form the staple article among a quantity of excellent small accessories made by this exhibitor, his luggage-frame for safeties being an astonishingly cheap line

at three shillings and sixpence, complete with straps, small handle-bar ; carriers with straps are sold as low as two shillings a pair.

189. **Crowe and Co.**—The registered cycle hose is the exhibit on their stall. We have worn this hose and can thoroughly recommend it. It is well made, comfortable and cheap.

190. **F. Cooke.**—In a musical country, the advantages of cycle bells which are musically toned should be appreciated. Such are the "Ulma" bells for which Mr. Cooke is the sole agent ; and the sounds they produce are not only musical, but sonorous, and they are made in a bewildering variety of patterns. We have been using "Ulmas" during the past winter, amid the noisy traffic of Dublin, and found them excellent signals as well as pleasant in tone,—free from the discordance of the average bicycle gong. Their varieties include single-stroke, double-stroke, and continuous-trill gongs, a singularly cheap line being a double-stroke gong selling at a shilling. The latest pattern takes the form of an improved clockwork gong, called the "Electra," wound up by a winch-handle on the top of the dome, and creating a tremendous din so long as the finger rests upon the handle ; it has also a continuous jingling attachment. A new patent band-clip is made of leather, to be tightened upon the handle-bar by a draw-screw. Another new pattern is a revolving gong, creating wonder as to where the ingenuity of inventors will stop ; its tone is at once loud, clear, and pleasantly musical. Among a great variety of other small accessories on this stand, are found such useful little notions as Hardy's chain-lubricator, costing only two shillings, for attachment to any cog-wheel ; an oil-controller to prevent waste or spilling of oil when filling lamp reservoirs or oil-cans, and several new kinds of screw wrenches, one of which, very similar to the old challenge wrench, differs from that in having a butterfly nut instead of a milled nut. "Ye Islington" lamp is so made that when laid down, or reversed, the oil will not distribute itself over the interior of the lamp, but will flow out of the reservoir into an external tube, whence it will return into the reservoir directly the lamp is righted.

191. **J. Prue.**—The "Chez-lui" hard-drying enamel has long enjoyed an enviable reputation as an excellent preparation with which repairs can be touched up, or the cyclist can re-enamel his own machine when the original black coating has worn shabby. To demonstrate the excellence of the poly-chromatic enamels of the same brand, a number of pretty stools are on view, coated entirely with æsthetic-tinted enamels and elegantly embellished with floral designs.

192. **H. A. Knox and Co.**—Lamps and lubricators, bags and bells, whistles and wrenches, carriers and cans, trumpets and toilet-cases, and all imaginable accessories, are sampled in a huge show-case emblematic of the extent of the business done in these goods by this enterprising firm.

193. **Patrick and Son.**—The "Cremorne" spring frame safety is the speciality of this firm. The frame is a semi-diamond, and it is hinged just behind the crank-axle bracket. Immediately above the axle of the rear wheel are placed two spiral springs on which the ends of the forks rest, and which give freely to all obstructions. Small rubber buffers are placed at each side so that even were the springs to break the ends of the forks would come down on these buffers, and the machine would thus be rideable. The spokes are butted, and can be ordered either direct or tangent. The machine seems a good practical anti-vibrator, and although so easy vertically, is rigid transversely. The price is £18 10s., and weight about

4olbs. The "Special Cremorne" has an immensely powerful frame. To all intents and purposes it is a diamond with cross stay, and a stout tube running from the cross stay to the centres. The crank-axle bracket is rigid. A lady's safety is made with drop frame and centre steering and hind wheel anti-vibrator.

194. **T. W. Tupper.**—The "Paragon" safety is a plain cross frame, listed at the marvellously low price of £6 6s. Another pattern is made with diamond frame; ball socket steering is fitted, and the price complete is £12 10s. A semi-diamond safety is also made.

195. **James Vallentine and Co.**—The "Spartan" safety No. 1 has a diamond frame with very rigid tread and centre steering. It is a good strong machine, and value at the price, £12 12s. The No. 2 has a diamond frame without cross stay and centre steering. There is sliding adjustment bracket, which is by no means too rigid. The No. 3 is a cross frame, stayed above and below, selling at £12 12s.; and the No. 4 sells at £10 10s.

196. **T. Redman and Co.**—The "Hero" safety has a strong well-stayed frame, with excellent tangent wheels, the spokes running direct through a flange in the hub without any bend, but the speciality about it is the spring fork, inside the front fork is fitted a false standard and fork in which the front wheel is fixed, the ends of the false fork slide in grooves in the front fork fitted with phosphor bronze guide blocks, whilst concealed in the front pillar is a stout coiled spring which receives the vibration of the false fork. Incidentally, another very important point is introduced in the shape of an arrangement whereby the pressure of the coiled spring can be increased or diminished by turning a milled wheel, and thus the anti-vibration arrangement can be made equally effective for a seven or sixteen stone rider. The idea seems good, and we should imagine, effective. Redman's improved home trainer is a simple stand for a safety, enabling the rider to practice on his own machine. The price complete is 13s. 9d. A novel single track sociable bicycle, invented by Mr. W. H. Smith, is shewn on this stall.

197. **Winnallie Cycle Co.**—The novelty of this exhibit is a spring-frame safety. The first main frame is divided near the saddle pillar, and is joined by a powerful coil spring which gives in the freest possible way when either wheel goes over an obstruction. It seems to act well and freely. A diamond frame safety is also shewn. It is well constructed, and rigid. A new idea for the brake is adopted. The fulcrum is placed on the far side of the steering post, and the spoon is applied by a tension rod, the advantages being greater leverage and a lighter rod. The idea is a good one. These machines are carefully and neatly built.

198. **The British Cycle Manufacturing Co.**—This firm exhibit so many patterns that it would be impossible to describe them all in the space at our disposal. They are plain, strong machines, at low prices, and mostly sold on the easy payment system. That they give satisfaction a host of testimonials testify. The original letters are pasted into books and arranged round the stall. There are no less than five of these books containing 250 testimonials each and one containing 550. We noted a cross-frame safety with 30in. driver and 36in. steerer stayed above and below and fitted with tangent-spokes, also a cross-frame safety with 30in. wheels, and a good-looking semi-diamond. The firm's diamond safety has a sliding bracket and socket steering, and a tricycle is shewn with a plain drop frame.

199. **Bennett and Bennett.**—A medium and a cheap class of safety find a home here, the "Tourists" being cross-framed substantial roadsters, one well stayed above and below, and the other only stayed between the crank bracket and the back-fork-ends. The saddle pillars terminate in cups covering their top ends, and carrying a socket in which the saddle-pin slides *behind* the pillar itself. The chain adjustment is effected by sliding the cup and tube bracket along a slotted projection in front of the back-fork end. Rim steel is used for the back stays. The Bennettini diamond framed safety has similar details to the others, but is tubular throughout.

200. **P. Wright.**—This South London maker's full roadster is a very perfect specimen of a safety, with a staunch square-angled crank bracket carrying the bearings outside the chain, 32 inch front and 30 inch back wheel, and a frame formed of triangles joined to a curved down-tube. A light roadster with cross-frame has the same square-cornered crank bracket, as also has the tricycle, the bracket in this case being a swing-action one to adjust the chain by the bridged stay-rods. The central pair of axle-bearings (of which there are four) are further stiffened by a semicircular piece of flat steel which passes behind the chain-wheel; and the very open drop frame has a detachable stay for a lady. They are all beautifully finished.

201. **W. A. Lloyd and Co.**—Hubs and other stampings, skeleton and complete frames, and wheels, are some of the ready-made parts with which Lloyd and Co. supply the trade, and the latest introduction takes the form of the "Bull-dog" spanner, the moving jaw of which takes an inner bearing as well as an outer purchase, upon the sides of the frame, thus relieving the adjusting screw of injurious strain.

202. **Leadbeater and Scott.**—An exceedingly neat show-case contained samples of the various kinds of steel so extensively supplied by this first-class Sheffield house to the cycle and engineering trades. Their files and tool-steel are particularly good.

203. **Goy, Limited.**—The club uniforms and general outfits associated with the name of Goy only need mentioning. The "perfecta" cycling shoe has been on the market longer than any other we know of, and should be so well tested by now as to justify its title.

204. **Hope Works Co.**—This exhibit comprised workshop appliances useful to makers and repairers, a new quick-acting bench vice deserving attention.

205. **Singer and Co.**—This is one of those old established firms who have already brought their cycles to such perfection, and who have commanded such an enormous patronage, that they have no necessity to alter in any radical manner their well-known patterns. Singer's machines are known as the strongest and most reliable made, and they have become popular through genuine merit and genuine merit alone. Their exhibit this year is remarkable for a reduction of weight and the introduction of some excellent contrivances. There is one which was exhibited last year, but which was not largely used during the season, and which consists of an arrangement for locking the steerer. It weighs very little and is so small and neat that it would hardly catch the eye, and yet, with a touch of the fingers, it locks the front wheel so that the machine can be left reclining against a wall in perfect safety. This is one of those things which should be on every safety, and we understand that the firm will let it out on royalty. Another introduction is the "Singer" spring fork. The fork is hinged to the rear of the front wheel spindle, and a strong spring just behind the shoulder of the

fork controls the play. Cone pins are used to take up the wear, and altogether the contrivance seems extremely effectual, and is wonderfully neat in appearance. Glancing over their exhibit, the first machine to strike our eye is the "Royal Singer" safety. The frame is the well-known semi-diamond introduced by this firm, with stay from the top of steering post carrying the saddle pillar. Ball steering is fitted, hollow rims, and a new hind wheel chain adjustment, and the machine is as pretty and neat looking a one as is to be found in the show; neither is the price, 18 guineas, extravagant for such an article. The weight has been wonderfully reduced, and is now well under 40lbs. Another pattern is made almost identical at 17 guineas. The No. 3 safety is an entirely new pattern. It has a diamond frame and centre steering with long centres. The spokes are butt-ended, as in the case of almost all "Singer's" machines, and the finish is admirable, and yet it sells at the low price of 15 guineas. The "Apollo" is also still to the fore and is listed at 14 guineas. The "Singer" Military safety is the machine which has been supplied to the Royal Irish Constabulary. It has the semi-diamond frame and is a very strong machine and most suitable for the purpose. A ladies' safety is built with an immensely powerful frame formed of parallel tubes. A tandem safety with a similar front frame is also constructed. In tricycles, the special "S. S. S." deserves close attention. It has the drop frame, with detachable stay, the upper end of the stay being secured to the top of the steering post, and the lower end can at will be secured to the seat pillar or to the main frame of the tricycle, should a lady wish to ride the machine. The wheels are 30in. and it will be hard to find a neater machine. The "S. S. S." No. 3 is a ladies' machine, with dropped frame strengthened with brackets at the angles. It is light though strong, and sells at 20 guineas. The firm show a specimen of this machine fitted with pneumatic tyres, a special neat fork getting over the clumsy appearance which some of the machines so fitted have. The "Singer's" tandem has now double ball steering. It has two brakes and is splendidly stayed, and is one of the few machines that have stood Irish roads. The No. 1 "S. S. S." is much as heretofore. The exhibit is altogether a grand one, and quite up to the firm's best form, which is saying a good deal.

206. Joseph Lucas and Son—This stall is simply covered with novelties. The world famous "King of the Road" lamp has been improved in several minor details. The front can now be detached for cleaning, and an arrangement does away with the slides for holding the oil reservoir; a cone-shaped projection from the inside of the lamp door fit into a hollow in the reservoir, securing it with a spring in the firmest possible manner. We should think this well-known lamp is now as near perfection as possible. The "Leader," a cheap pattern with the same improvements, sells at 10s. 6d. The "Edison" is a new introduction, and has a fixed reflector, but in other respects is similar to the former patterns, though the finish is not quite so good. It sells at 9s. 6d. The "Popular" sells at 7s. 6d., and the "Planet" the cheapest make of Messrs. Lucas, at 4s. The firm have much improved their new clip for bells, which now will fit any sized handle-bar. They have bought Messrs. Challis's business in this line, and have very much improved the Challis bell. They also bring out a cheap specimen at 2s. 6d., and a plain little bell at 1s. Cycleorns are also exhibited. A new oil-can has been introduced. For the safety the "Stop Thief"—an old tricyclist's invention—has once more been put on the market. It consists simply of a bar of metal with a T piece at the end, and

a hole for a padlock at the other end which, being slipped through the chain and the padlock fastened, secures it firmly. The price is 1s. The firm have also put on the market a really splendid luggage carrier at 5s. It is secured with the new clips, and is simply full of strap holes, so that parcels of all sizes can be carried. A very useful bag is made for this particular carrier. It can be slipped on or taken off without a moment's delay. The "King's Own" handle-bar carrier is also shown, and tins of enamel and oil are made a speciality. A patent toe clip struck us most favourably, being both easily and quickly applied, and selling at 2s. 6d. The firm have brought out three new wrenches. The "Gripper" being a specially good one, catching the nut on three sides, hence its name. They have also improved and made very much lighter the Cripper lamp-bracket. Altogether their stall well repaid close inspection.

207. Cellular Clothing Co.—On this stall is displayed a large selection of cycling shirts, hose, and underclothing generally, made of the cellular stuff from which the compny takes its name. They claim that by wearing this stuff, the cyclist gains the same advantage as if he wore all wool, and that it is cheaper to buy and pleasanter to the skin.

208. Foley and Webb.—This firm are very large makers of saddles, and on their stall we find a new saddle divided at the peak, and also Von Lubbes patent saddle which is divided at the back. They have also secured the right to manufacture the famous "Lilliebridge" American saddle, which bears a reputation of being the most comfortable made. We once had an opportunity of trying one for a short period and were greatly pleased with it. Pouches, and oils, and luggage carriers, and accessories of all kinds are also shown.

209. Charles White.—"Electrine" cycle oil is the speciality of Mr. White. It bears the highest reputation as being one of the brightest burning oils made, and we hope shortly to have an opportunity of testing it fully, when we shall have something more to say about its quality. It is made of two separate descriptions, one for burning and the other for lubricating, and is put up in convenient square tins with lips at the corners for conveniently filling oilcans and reservoirs; and to facilitate handling, the tins are furnished with a loop of leather at the top.

210. East London Rubber Co.—Tyres, rubber pedals, waterproofs, and rubber goods generally are shown in great profusion.

211. Rudge Cycle Co.—This well known firm completely occupy the Egyptian Court with their large and varied exhibit. A very large number of safeties are exhibited. The Bicyclette No 1 is much the same as last year. It is a thoroughly well stayed machine, with neat swing bracket, and the rear chain wheel is secured outside the fork or in the usual position, according to the fancy of the customer. A cheaper pattern is made at £14. A new introduction this year is the diamond frame. It is of the most approved pattern, with strong cross stay and centre steering and swing bracket. This is a really nice machine, finished in the best style at £18, a low price for such a very high class article. The No. 2 of the same pattern, struck us as about the most useful introduction on the stand. The frame is constructed throughout of double tubes, the crank axle bearings being secured at the angles, so that the tread is as rigid as it can be. In fact a better frame could not be constructed. The steering is centre, and the general appearance of the machine is that of the very highest grade article, and yet it sells at the very moderate price of £14. We have seen no better value in the show, and would strongly advise our Irish readers to keep this machine in mind, and to call and have a look at it at the Stephen's Street depôt as soon as it is stocked. It should be just the thing for our roads. The "Bicyclette" tandem is a magnificently stayed machine with perfectly rigid brackets. By the removal of a stay from seat pillar to neck, it can be adapted for a lady on the front seat. The firm also make a racer of this pattern, which is stayed in every possible way, and still exceedingly light. A ladies' safety is shown, which is admirably suited for the purpose for which it is designed. Already some of them are running in Dublin, and giving satisfaction. Perhaps one of the greatest novelties shown by the firm is their new spring frame. In appearance the machine is somthing like a cross-framed safety. The rear portion of the frame consists of a triangle, which can play freely round the hind wheel spindle, and which is not fixed in any way to the backbone, but rises and falls independently of it, the play being regulated by a plunger working in a cylinder and a stiff spring. The arrangement is very neat and effectual, as we know by personal experience, for recently in Coventry we had a run of some miles on this machine, and found it exceedingly easy over rough surfaces. An ant-vibration handlebar is also fixed, which is simplicity itself. The handle is hinged with a very strong spring keeping it in place, and the effect is that when the front wheel strikes an obstacle the spring is compressed, and the wheel rises without any movement of the hands taking place. A tricycle is also exhibited with the spring frame. It has a forked backbone like the safety, and is extremely neat and simple in appearance, and we should imagine that in this connection the action of the spring would be even better than on the safety. The Rudge No. 1 tricycle has been considerably improved in design and detail. A stay has been added from seat pillar to neck, and other little improvements introduced which go far to make the machine perfect. The No. 2 is different in outline, but is a really good machine, and sells at £18 18s. Both No. 1 and No. 2 tandems are exhibited splendidly stayed ; in fact there is not a better stayed machine in the show than the No. 1. Of course the great attraction of this exhibit is "Phillip's Triplet"—a machine which has proved itself the fastest, bar none. The frame cannot be stronger, every possible strain and stress is provided for, and being a two-tracker it should be admirably suited for Irish roads. The steering is perfection, and the machine is most suitable for two ladies. It is also made as a tandem, and we believe runs very well as such. The "Rudge" sociable closely resembles two safeties joined together side by side. It looks an exceedingly strong and comfortable machine, but we have never had an opportunity of trying it.

212. **Charles Mackintosh and Co.**—Tyres, pedal rubbers, handles, and rubber goods generally, are exhibited.

213. **Samuel Snell and Co.**—The "Unique" lamp is still to the fore with its patent spring ball arrangement. We have used this lamp and can testify as to its merits. Another pattern that the firm have just introduced is the "Arlington," in which the glass protrudes at the upper end so as to throw the light more down on the ground, and which is fitted either with links or the spring ball arrangement. The "Sydenham" is an entirely new pattern. Although this lamp is not a large one, the oil reservoir is of greater capacity than is found in most other lamps, and in appearance it is extremely neat. On this stall also are found a great variety of wrenches, bells, saddles, springs, tyre-fixers, and other accessories similar to those exhibited last year.

214. **Scottish Sports Agency.**—Here are to be found copies of our contemporaries, *The Scottish Cyclist* and *Scotch Sport*, the principal cycling organs of North Britain.

215. **Walker Watch Co.**—The "Walker" watches are here shown with clips for attaching them to cycle lamps for the use of road scorchers and others who wish to see how time flies without the trouble of taking out their watch.

216. **J. Butler.**—Cycling accessories of all kinds are here shown. A very neat cylindrical pocket oil can struck us favourably.

217. **W. S. Loudon.**—Tyre Cement is the speciality of Mr. Loudon, and in his own particular line he holds pride of place, supplying wholesale quantities to a great number of the foremost cyclemakers.

218. **John Harrison.**—The "Kensington" lamp requires no description, it is already so well and favourably known. The firm exhibit all kinds of accessories, but they seem to have very few novelties, and as their goods are already well known, we need not dilate on them. We note a neat pedal clip, also a detachable lamp bracket, and the "Kensington" lamp up to date, which appears a really good article. Their continuous alarms and other bells well deserve notoriety, and in pedals, hubs and safety fittings, bottom brackets, spanners, whistles, saddles, and other accessories they are second to none.

219. **H. Miller and Co.**—Good wine needs no bush, and "Bell Rock" Lamp is so well known in Ireland that it hardly requires a description. It has been remodelled so that the details are somewhat different, but it still possesses all its old features. the "Bell Rock" whistle to be attached to the handlebar, and blown by means of a rubber ball is also shown. The form has also brought out a new brake holder, and contrivance to be fitted to the inside of a spoon brake so as to give it a better grip. Their watch carrier for attachment to a lamp is very neat. They have a new adjustible wrench of very perfect design. Luggage carriers, patent spanners, cycle horns, whistles, and hundreds of other accessories are shown.

220. **Lamplugh and Brown.**—A very tasty and well got up exhibit is that of the famous saddle makers. In saddles this year they have not gone in for a variety, but those they show are really good. They are adopting the three coil spring combination very generally, the spring being interchangeable and the tilt can be easily regulated as also the tension of the saddle and they have shown their wisdom in making this their standard pattern, for their is no better in the show. The "Scorcher" is a very light pattern with a mere apology for a spring and built to meet the wants of road scorchers. Saddles are also offered for boys and youths. Perhaps the greatest novelty on their stall is the pneumatic handle which if it fulfils our expectation should be attached to every cycle made. Its use on which should at all events go a long way to deaden the disagreeable vibration caused by the front wheel of a safety. Merit rather than variety is the characteristic of this exhibit and it is none the less interesting on this account.

221. **A. Paine.**—A very nice exhibit of remarkably light and well-finished machines is that of this maker. The "Demon" roadster is the first machine we noticed. It has the cross-frame strongly stayed above and below, and with centre steering. It is nicely finished and turned out in every respect, and scales under 40lbs. The Irish "Demon," a stronger pattern, with double front stay and a very rigid bracket and tangent spokes, is listed at £18. 18s. The "Demon" light roadster has a peculiar frame—it is

triangular behind and rectangular in front ; the steering is ball socket and the tread rigid. It is an exceedingly well-designed machine, and the maker states that it is only 27lbs. weight. The racer is of the same pattern, and is said to be only 19lbs. The "Demon" second grade roadster is a cross-frame, well stayed, with rigid tread and tangent spokes. It is an excellent looking mount, and cheapness itself at £14. A light roadster, with cross-frame stayed above and below, is built at 26lbs. These machines have a good local reputation, and are ridden by such men as Jones, Price and Shute, of the Polytechnic ; and when in Scotland last year we saw the Five Miles N.C.U. Championship there won on a "Demon."

222. Metropolitan Machinists Co.—A large exhibit of machines, possessing no very special features. The "Juno" No 1 is a cross frame with centre steering, swing bracket, and tangent spokes. The "Juno" diamond frame is of the popular pattern with centre steering, and the steering post is hinged just under the centres, so as to absorb the vibration. Price 15 guineas. A ladies' safety is made, fitted with this spring arrangement. The No. 5 safety is strongly stayed above and below with square swing frame bracket. Their No 8 is a diamond frame pattern with centre steering. Another pattern is made with socket steering. The No. 10 is a cross frame, stayed above and below, and selling at £10 10s. The "Juno" tricycle has the drop frame with strengthening bracket, and sells at £20. Other patterns are made at prices ranging from 11 guineas upwards.

223. S. and B. Gorton, Limited.—Another exhibit of strong and reliable-looking safeties. The No. 10 has a semi-diamond frame with forward stay and centre-steering, and a sliding crank-axle bracket. It is built on good lines and looks its value for £13. The No. 11 has the popular diamond frame with centre-steering, and either tangent or direct spokes. It is a strong rigid-looking machine and sells at £13 10s. No. o has a semi-diamond frame and is finished in superior style with tangent wheels. It is listed at 16 guineas. The No. 2 is a very strong-looking cross-frame with forward stay and centre-steering. It is a staunch-looking roadster and sells at £12. A youth's machine with a swing bracket is turned out at £7 10s., and a ladies' safety with strengthening bracket at the angle and a detachable stay in case a gentleman should desire to use it, is listed at £14. These machines all seem strong and serviceable.

224. The London Cycle Manufacturing Co.—An astonishingly well finished and light exhibit, and evidently turned out with the most careful attention to details. The "North Road" safety is a semi-diamond frame, with ball socket head and light tangent spokes. It is nicely finished and has slot adjustment. It is exceedingly light, considering the strength. The design "B" has the diamond frame, the cross stay being made of double tubing ; the bracket is rigid, and the steering socket. The ball races are brought well out, and througout the machine is admirably constructed. The weight is 35lbs. Design "C" is officially certified by Mr. Dring to be only 23lbs. weight, and this takes the cake as the lightest road machine in the show. It has an extremely rigid frame, and the handles are brought nicely back. A safety is made for ladies with strengthening bracket and detachable stay. The "London" safety at £12 is marvellous value. It has a cross-frame stayed above and below, and socket steering, and scales all on well under 40lbs. A tricycle is made with drop frame and detachable stay and ball socket head, scaling 41lbs. It is a nice machine,

listed at £22 1s. An ordinary is also shown with ball socket head, which is a decided novelty.

225 Rickard and Dods.—Three exceedingly light and nicely finished patterns of the "Westminster" safety are shown by this firm. The "A" has semi-diamond frame with double tubular stay from crank-axle bracket to steering post. The steering-socket and all the details are carefully attended to. Weight under 30lbs. The "B," a diamond-frame made of double tubes throughout and exceedingly rigid. Weight under 40lbs. Price £15 10s. ; a grand machine for the money. The "C" has a cross-frame with tubular stays above and below and socket-steering. Also a grand machine for the price, £15 10s. The exhibit, though small, was a good one.

226. Sydney Lee.—The Cortis safety is here shown. It is a beautifully designed machine with diamond frame, the tubing from centre to rear wheel being double. A slot adjustment is used, and both the frame and crank-axle bracket are exceedingly rigid. Keen's pedals are fitted. Another pattern diamond is made with double tubing throughout, and a swing bracket and a decided novelty is introduced in the front portion of the machine, the steering centres being put in front of the steering post, and a spring fork used to deaden the vibration. A quadricycle for one rider is also shown.

228. The Maeda Vale Cycle Company.—The No. 1, "Eiffel" is a diamond-framed safety with double tubing with the exception of the upper side. The chain tension is adjusted by means of a sliding bracket. It is exceedingly rigid ; ball-socket is fitted. The machine is a nice-looking mount, listed at £16. The No. 2 has centre-steering, but otherwise is like the No. 1. It is listed at 12 guineas.

229. H. Sims. The "Universal" Safety has a diamond frame with cross stay and ball socket-steering. The tread is rigid, and the chain tension adjusted by sliding the rear wheel spindle on the fork ends. A diamond-frame tricycle is also shown, and an intensely rigid and well-stayed tandem.

230. J. M. Hale.—Hale's patent water-cycle is here shown. It consists of a long racing-gig kind of boat driven by paddles worked by the feet, and it looks practicable though the weight must be considerable.

The above report is as perfect as time would permit, and we desire to express our thanks to the various exhibitors for the trouble they took in pointing out the novelties to us. Of course there were exceptions, and in some such cases the reports are necessarily short owing to the difficulty of grasping the various "points" without help in the time at our disposal. In other cases a short report is due to the fact that the machines of the firms under notice have given such general satisfaction that they have not seen fit to make many alterations in their last year's patterns. The St. George's Engineering Co., and a few more of the leading makers, are cases in point, and our readers will, therefore, bear in mind that a short or long report is not, *per se*, any criterion as to the merits of the machines. In case we have omitted anything of importance, we shall, with great pleasure, publish the particulars in next weekly issue if exhibitor will kindly call our attention to the omission.

In subsequent issues of the IRISH CYCLIST AND ATHLETE we hope to give illustrated descriptions of some of the greatest novelties at the Show. Readers of this special number should not miss these.